## Identification & Value Guide

# DEPRESSION ERA GLASSWARE

## 4th EDITION

# Carl F. Luckey

Published by

**krause
publications**

700 E. State Street • Iola, WI 54990-0001
Telephone: 715/445-2214

Please call or write for our free catalog.
Our toll-free number to place an order or obtain a free catalog is 800-258-0929
or please use our regular business telephone 715-445-2214
for editorial comment and further information.

Library of Congress Catalog Number: 2001099522
ISBN: 0-89689-104-6

Depression glass pieces featured on the front cover are, top row, from left: Pitcher and tumbler,
Hobnail; 4-ounce tumbler, allover Cherry Blossom, pink; and green covered butter dish, Georgian (Love Birds).
Bottom row, from left, are: dinner plate, 10-1/2", Lace Edge, pink; large plate,
American Sweetheart, monax; and 60-ounce water pitcher, 8" high, Princess.

Pieces on the back cover are, clockwise from top right: 5-1/2" high tumbler and 10.2" high footed pitcher,
Floral (Poinsettia), green; 5" diameter fruit bowl, 6-3/4" diameter plate, and 10-1/2" long oval bowl,
Rosemary (Dutch Rose), amber; and 5-3/4" high goblet, 9 ounces, Mayfair, pink.

Printed in the United States of America

# In Memoriam

## *Carl F. Luckey*
## *(1941-1998)*

Sadly, author and friend Carl F. Luckey passed away prior to the publication of this, the fourth edition of **Depression Era Glassware**. Those who knew Carl are well aware that he touched many lives beyond the scope of his books. Carl was, in fact, a genuine hero, an ambitious volunteer, and a patron of the arts.

A Nashville native and resident of Killen, Alabama, at the time of his death, Carl will be remembered for far greater deeds than the more than 25 books he had expertly written. He was a decorated Air Force pilot who earned the Distinguished Flying Cross and National Defense Medal during the Vietnam War. Carl was later an active civic volunteer and member of the United States Coast Guard Auxiliary. In 1995, he received The Plaque of Merit from the Coast Guard for preventing the loss of life at the risk of his own. He was also an active seaman and pillar of his community.

Carl was 57 when he unexpectedly died in November of 1998, leaving behind a loving wife, Mary Frances. Carl's legacy lives on, yet he is, and will continue to be, missed by the many who knew him.

— Krause Publications

# ACKNOWLEDGMENTS

Krause Publications extends a special note of appreciation to Depression glass consultants Debbie and Randy Coe of Hillsboro, Oregon. Without their insight, valued opinions, and expert contributions, this new edition would not have been possible.

Debbie and Randy are board members of the Pacific Northwest Fenton Association—he is president and she is show chairwoman. They are also columnists for *Old Stuff* and *Antique Quarterly*, both area antiques newspapers, and occasionally write articles for *West Coast Peddler*, a California antiques newspaper. In addition, Randy helps at several identification booths at antiques shows in the Oregon area.

Krause Publications extends a thank you to the following people who also provided their expertise: Victor and Dianne Elliot, Debbie Lane, Swede and Kay Larson, Seaside Antique Mall and Blue Ribbon Photography.

# CONTENTS

# INTRODUCTION

## Depression Glass

There is a book available that curiously predicts that Depression glass, among other things, is a collectible of tomorrow. The author is sadly mistaken. It is a collectible of today, most assuredly.

Depression glass came into being in the 1920s and what we call Depression glass is more accurately labeled Depression era glass. It is glassware made from just a few years before the Great Depression through and on into the 1940s, although some glassware included in the broad category of Depression glass is still being produced. Most of it is characterized by a machine-molded design incorporating design patterns that are often very intricately detailed, but also occur in optic and/or geometric motifs.

The colors used are another very distinctive characteristic of this glassware. The product was manufactured to be cheap, frequently on order to be given away as advertising or promotional premiums. Some have even said the colors were used to disguise what would otherwise appear to be imperfect, bubbled, and streaked glass. Whether this is true is open to argument. Whatever the reasons, the colors used are distinctive and, at times, striking in intensity and depth. Most characteristically, it is found in varying transparent hues of pink, green, blue, yellow, or clear glass with no color at all, referred to as "crystal" by dealers and collectors. There were, of course, many other colors used, but those listed above are the most common.

## About the Values in This Book

You will immediately note, upon looking at the pattern listings, that the values of the items listed are presented in ranges. This is a more realistic approach to valuation because that is what you will run into when buying. Values can vary greatly from dealer to dealer and region to region.

The values given are here and now, at the time this book was being updated, and represent an opinion derived from today's market and many years of dealer experience. The value ranges are a **guide**; nothing more.

Values presented in this book are useful only when used in conjunction with several other value guides, price lists, etc., and the experience level of the user. People have a tendency to jump right into price lists upon obtaining books such as this, with no regard to the introductory material, and to use these value guides as the final word—their value bible, as it were. They select this or any other guide as a quick and final answer. The people who use the guides most effectively are those who view them only as one of the four or five other factors that should be considered in each specific instance where one needs to evaluate an item for sale or purchase.

## Restoration or Repair

Condition of pieces is a factor influencing value. If a particular item is badly scratched and chipped, it will very likely fall far below the lower figure in the value range for it.

If an item has only small or one or two chips or scratches, it can fairly easily be repaired by a competent craftsman specializing in this type of work. These people can also repair broken stems and such. Many times the repairs are flawless and undetectable.

Because of the relative abundance of many patterns and the requirement of only a small outlay for most, I don't consider well-repaired or restored items as worthless or worth less than the same non-damaged item. Ethically, however, those that have been repaired should always be presented as such.

One last word: It may be cheaper just to buy a replacement, if you can find it. In the case of repairs, look before you leap.

## Reissues, Reproductions, and Fakes

Fortunately, Depression era glassware is, in the main, an inexpensive collectible. There are, however, a few exceptions. To see an extraordinary exception, turn to the Mayfair ("Open Rose") pattern by Hocking and look over the figures in the value listing.

If you have looked at the pages mentioned above and recovered sufficiently from the shock, I will try to relieve your mind by reiterating: Collecting Depression glass is an inexpensive hobby if you shop wisely and employ at least a modicum of patience.

Now, in view of the lofty prices of the "Open Rose" pattern, we must discuss an ugly problem. In any area of collecting, when some of the items are rare and/or avidly sought, there are some who will attempt to take advantage of it. There are several different ways to profit by the popularity or rarity of various patterns and specific items of Depression glass. These run the full spectrum from honest profit motives to downright dishonesty.

As you read through the pattern discussions, you will come across a few (very few) instances where the company that originated the pattern in the 1920s or 1930s is still in business and is either still producing it or, worse, **has reissued the old pattern using the original molds**. That this is a matter of their prerogative and that it is quite honest is a foregone conclusion. After all, they own the design and molds. My argument with this is not new or original, but it is nonetheless valid. I join the ranks of the others in objecting to this practice as a disservice to collectors and, indirectly, to the very companies doing it. The company is in the business of making money, of course, and taking advantage of a potentially profitable market situation, by definition, makes money. What the companies don't realize is the very real presence of another market situation: the millions of consumers who collect Depression glass. To illustrate this, suppose the original company was to reissue the entire line of the expensive Mayfair pattern. That would not only make the collectors of that pattern hopping mad, but the event would make headlines across the country in all the collector publications. Now, that represents bad media exposure to millions of people. If that wouldn't drive the company's public-relations director to the brink, I don't know what would. The solution to the dilemma of reissues is a simple one and I wonder that it is not often used. All the reissuing company has to do is mark the items in such a way as to make it obvious that it is, indeed, a reissue: placing a date or mark in the mold to make the reissue easy to spot.

The scenario painted above is admittedly extreme, but clearly the practice of reissuing has to have some impact on the company, however small.

Jumping to the other end of the spectrum, we find ourselves face to face with that nefarious character, the crook. This vulture in the blue sky of collecting can swoop down on you in several forms: the dishonest dealer, the thief, the deceiver, and the fake or forger. The dishonest dealer is fairly rare, but the crook in concert (knowingly or unknowingly) with the forger is a clear and present danger.

A recent collector periodical carried an article about a lady showing up at a show with a "family heirloom." She went from dealer to dealer carrying a "Miss America" butter dish (value range: $188 to $425, depending upon color), offering it for sale. Some bit and bought; others balked. It was a reproduction or a fake. I don't presume to judge whether it was an intentional fake or a legitimate (?) reproduction, but that the woman was a thief, there can be no doubt.

The balking dealers knew their stuff and so must you. You have to study, learn, and experience your hobby.

There have been just a few of these reproductions and fakes to show up so far and they are listed and described in detail in this book for you. They are discussed with each pattern in which they occur.

There are many other items of Depression glass that could be attractive to interested shady individuals, so arm yourself with knowledge.

## Pattern Listing

The following section is the pattern identification guide. It is arranged alphabetically according to the pattern name most often used, either official company nomenclature, or, in the absence of that, the name given and used most often by collectors.

Under each listing, you will find the company that produced the pattern, the colors you might find in the pattern, and a description of the pattern, with some history and rarities to be found.

When there are reproductions or reissues known, they are discussed as well.

The last category to appear with each listing is the pattern value range chart.

## Pattern Index

Included in this book is an alphabetical listing of all pattern names or nicknames that are, or have been, used to facilitate ease of location. For example, if you are in the habit of calling "Cameo" by the name "Ballerina" or "Dancing Girl," you will find it listed all three ways in the index.

# ADAM

### 1932 - 1934

Jeannette Glass Company                    Jeannette, Pennsylvania

**Colors found to date:**

- Crystal
  - Topaz (rare)
- Green
- Pink
- Yellow (very rare)

# ADAM

## Reproductions or reissues

So far, there is only one piece in the Adam line that is known to have been reproduced. The covered butter dish in pink has only been offered by A. A. Importing Company, Inc. It is 6 inches across and the only way to really tell the new from the old is to be familiar with the look of genuine Depression era pink. The new piece has a pink color that has a decidedly "washed out" or "watery" look in comparison.

## General pattern notes

Sometimes the collector may encounter the factory trademark of a "J" enclosed in a triangle, but this occurs so infrequently, it is an unreliable indicator.

The color most commonly found in the Adam pattern is pink. It is also the most popularly collected color.

Variations to look for are the pitchers found with both round and square bases, butter dishes whose lids are found with the Adam pattern, or a combination of the Adam with the Sierra pattern on the lids. So far, the latter variation is found only in pink. The Sierra design is on the outside and the Adam design is on the inside.

Candy and sugar lids are identical.

| ITEM & DESCRIPTION | DOLLAR VALUE RANGES BY COLOR | |
|---|---|---|
| | Pink | Green |
| Ashtray, 4-1/2" | 28-30 | 24-26 |
| Bowl, 4-3/4" | 20-24 | 20-24 |
| Bowl, 5-3/4" | 45-50 | 40-45 |
| Bowl, 7-3/4" | 28-30 | 25-28 |
| Bowl (covered), 9" | 85-95 | 95-110 |
| Bowl (oval), 10" | 34-40 | 36-38 |
| Butter dish and cover | 110-125 | 350-400 |
| Butter dish (combination "Sierra" pattern) | 1,400-1,500 | — |
| Cake plate (footed), 10" | 35-38 | 38-40 |
| Candlesticks (pair), 4" | 85-95 | 100-125 |
| Candy jar and cover | 125-135 | 135-150 |
| Coaster, 3-1/4" | 20-22 | 18-20 |
| Creamer | 18-20 | 18-20 |
| Cup | 24-28 | 22-24 |
| Lamp | 350-375 | 375-400 |
| Pitcher, 8" | 60-70 | 70-80 |
| Pitcher (round base), 32 oz. | 95-100 | 70-80 |
| Plate, 6" | 10-12 | — |
| Plate (square), 7-3/4" | 16-22 | 12-14 |
| Plate (square), 9" | 24-26 | 26-28 |
| Plate (grill), 9" | 20-24 | 18-20 |
| Platter, 11-3/4" | 35-38 | 40-45 |
| Relish dish (sectioned), 8" | 20-24 | 24-26 |
| Salt and pepper (footed), 4" | 75-85 | 95-125 |
| Saucer (square), 6" | 5-8 | 5-9 |
| Sherbet | 28-30 | 30-32 |
| Sugar | 18-20 | 18-20 |
| Sugar or candy cover | 28-30 | 35-40 |
| Tumbler, 4-1/2" | 40-45 | 35-40 |
| Tumbler, 5-1/2" | 75-85 | 65-75 |
| Vase, 7-1/2" | 295-325 | 100-125 |

# AMERICAN PIONEER

### 1931 - 1934

Liberty Works                                   Egg Harbor, New Jersey

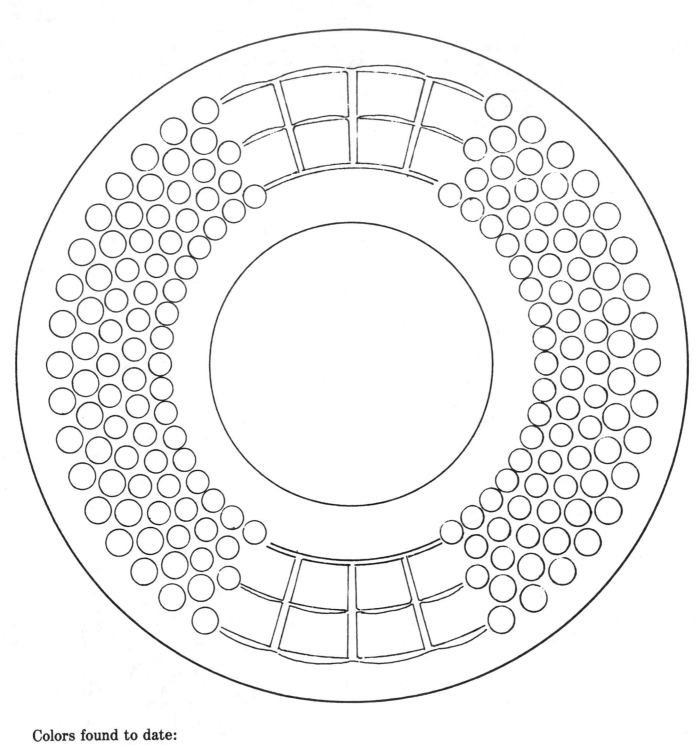

Colors found to date:

- Amber          • Crystal          • Green          • Pink

# AMERICAN PIONEER

## Reproductions or reissues

None are known.

## General pattern notes

This is one of the more uncommon patterns, as can be readily seen by some of the values listed below. Early Liberty Works advertisements state: "Each piece will carry an embossed paper label worded 'American Pioneer, by Liberty'," but these are seldom seen. About the only way the collector might find a piece with the label intact would be if he were fortunate enough to stumble upon some unsold boxed stock in a dark and dusty corner.

Green is the most popularly collected color, followed quite closely by pink. Amber is the rare color and crystal follows far behind pink and green in popularity.

Rare pieces are the whiskey jigger and the post-Prohibition 3-ounce wine goblets. Also difficult to locate are the 8-ounce water goblets and the two sizes of covered bowls.

| ITEM & DESCRIPTION | DOLLAR VALUE RANGES BY COLOR | | |
|---|---|---|---|
| | Crystal | Green | Pink |
| Bowl, 5" (handled) | 11-13 | 14-16 | 12-14 |
| Bowl, 8-3/4" (covered) | 85-95 | 110-125 | 24-26 |
| Bowl, 9" (handled) | 21-14 | 28-30 | 24-26 |
| Bowl, 9-1/4" (covered) | 80-85 | 110-125 | 95-110 |
| Bowl, 10-3/8" (console) | 40-44 | 65-70 | 50-60 |
| Candlesticks, 6-1/2" (pair) | 50-55 | 85-95 | 75-85 |
| Candy jar and cover (small) | 75-80 | 100-125 | 85-95 |
| Candy jar and cover (large) | 80-85 | 125-145 | 100-125 |
| Cheese and cracker set (indented plate and compote) | 30-35 | 45-50 | 40-45 |
| Coaster, 3-1/2" | 28-30 | 30-35 | 28-30 |
| Creamer (small) | 18-20 | 24-26 | 22-24 |
| Creamer (large) | 18-20 | 24-26 | 22-24 |
| Cup | 8-10 | 16-18 | 14-16 |
| Dresser set (two colognes, power jar, 7-1/2" tray) | 145-165 | — | 275-325 |
| Goblet, 4" | 28-30 | 42-45 | 35-40 |
| Goblet, 6" | 35-40 | 45-50 | 35-40 |
| Ice bucket, 6" | 45-50 | 65-70 | 60-65 |
| Lamp (ball shaped) (amber: 55-77) | 85-90 | — | 90-100 |
| Lamp, 8-1/2" | 95-110 | 145-160 | 125-145 |
| Pitcher, 5" (covered) (amber: 250-330) | 145-160 | 195-225 | 175-195 |
| Pitcher, 7" (covered) (amber: 250-330) | 165-175 | 225-245 | 195-225 |
| Plate, 8" | 8-10 | 12-14 | 10-12 |
| Plate, 11-1/2" (handled) | 20-22 | 26-30 | 24-26 |
| Saucer | 3-5 | 10-12 | 4-6 |
| Sherbet, 3-1/2" | 10-12 | 16-18 | 14-16 |
| Sherbet, 4-3/4" | 20-24 | 30-35 | 28-30 |
| Sugar, 2-3/4" | 18-20 | 24-26 | 22-24 |
| Sugar, 3-1/2" | 18-20 | 24-26 | 14-16 |
| Tumbler, 3-1/2", 5 oz. | 20-24 | 32-35 | 28-32 |
| Tumbler, 4", 8 oz. | 22-24 | 28-30 | 26-28 |
| Tumbler, 5", 12 oz. | 24-26 | 36-40 | 34-36 |
| Vase, 4-1/4" (footed rose bowl) | 55-65 | 90-100 | 55-65 |
| Vase, 7" (four styles) | 50-60 | 125-135 | 75-85 |
| Whiskey jigger, 2-1/4" | 40-45 | 60-65 | 55-60 |

# AMERICAN SWEETHEART

1930 - 1936

Macbeth-Evans Glass Company                    Charleroi, Pennsylvania

Colors found to date:

- Cremax          • Dark Blue          • Monax
- Pink            • Ruby red           • Smoke

# AMERICAN SWEETHEART

**Reproductions or reissues**

None are known.

**General pattern notes**

American Sweetheart is probably one of the most popular of the Macbeth-Evans pattern lines. The name was given the pattern by collectors, as the company referred to it as its "R Pattern." It originally appeared in pink, but soon became available in other colors. The monax pieces are sometimes found with colored rims, and the very rare smoke is always found black-rimmed.

The patterns are found both on the front and reverse sides and sometimes a combination of sides. Sometimes on the monax pieces, the center portion of the design is omitted altogether. Incidentally, if you find a gold-rimmed monax piece, it is dated 1935 (the year the gold rim was added) or later. Pitchers and tumblers have so far been found in pink only.

Pitchers and salt/pepper shakers are the most difficult pieces to find in this pattern.

This is one of the very few patterns that also presents sherbets with no stem or base. The sherbets are made to fit into a metal base.

| ITEM & DESCRIPTION | DOLLAR VALUE RANGES BY COLOR | | | | | |
|---|---|---|---|---|---|---|
| | Cremax | Monax | Blue | Pink | Red | Smoke |
| Bowl, 3-3/4" | — | — | — | 75-85 | — | — |
| Bowl, 4-1/2" (cream soup) | — | 95-125 | — | 85-95 | — | — |
| Bowl, 6" | 14-16 | 16-18 | — | 16-18 | — | 30-35 |
| Bowl, 9" (round) | 46-56 | 65-70 | — | 60-65 | — | 80-90 |
| Bowl, 9-1/2" (flat soup) | — | 95-100 | — | 85-95 | — | — |
| Bowl, 11" (oval) | — | 85-95 | — | 75-85 | — | — |
| Bowl, 18" (console) | — | 450-500 | 1,350-1,500 | — | 1,300-1,400 | — |
| Creamer (footed) | — | 20-24 | 145-175 | 18-20 | 185-195 | 70-80 |
| Cup | — | 21-24 | 120-145 | 18-20 | 145-160 | 50-60 |
| Lampshade | 550-600 | 650-700 | — | — | — | — |
| Plate, 6" | — | 4-6 | — | 6-8 | — | 15-20 |
| Plate, 8" | — | 10-12 | 100-125 | 12-14 | 125-145 | 30-35 |
| Plate, 9" | — | 12-14 | — | — | — | 35-40 |
| Plate, 9-3/4" | — | 40-45 | — | 35-40 | — | 60-65 |
| Plate, 10-1/4" | — | 30-35 | — | 35-40 | — | — |
| Plate, 11" | — | 20-24 | — | — | — | — |
| Plate, 12" (salver) | — | 26-28 | 300-350 | 24-26 | 350-375 | — |
| Plate, 15-1/2" | — | 275-300 | 450-495 | — | 425-450 | — |
| Platter, 13" (oval) | — | 75-85 | — | 65-75 | — | 125-145 |
| Pitcher, 7-1/2" | — | — | — | 850-950 | — | — |
| Pitcher, 8" | — | — | — | 750-850— | — | — |
| Salt and pepper (footed) | — | 400-450 | — | 600-650 | — | — |
| Saucer | — | 6-8 | 25-30 | 5-6 | 20-25 | 15-20 |
| Sherbet, 4" (footed) | — | — | — | 20-24 | — | — |
| Sherbet, 4-1/4" (footed) | — | 22-26 | — | 18-22 | — | 40-45 |
| Sherbet in metal holder (crystal only: 5-9) | — | — | — | — | — | — |
| Sugar (footed, no cover) | — | 21-24 | 145-175 | 18-20 | 175-195 | 70-80 |
| Sugar cover (monax only) | — | 250-300 | — | — | — | — |
| Tidbit (three level, 8", 12", 15-1/2") | | — | 250-300 | 800-850 | — | 650-700 |
| Tumbler, 3-1/2" | — | — | — | 90-100 | — | — |
| Tumbler, 4" | — | — | — | 85-95 | — | — |
| Tumbler, 4-1/2" | — | — | — | 110-125 | — | — |

# ANNIVERSARY

**1947 - 1949**

Jeannette Glass Company                  Jeannette, Pennsylvania

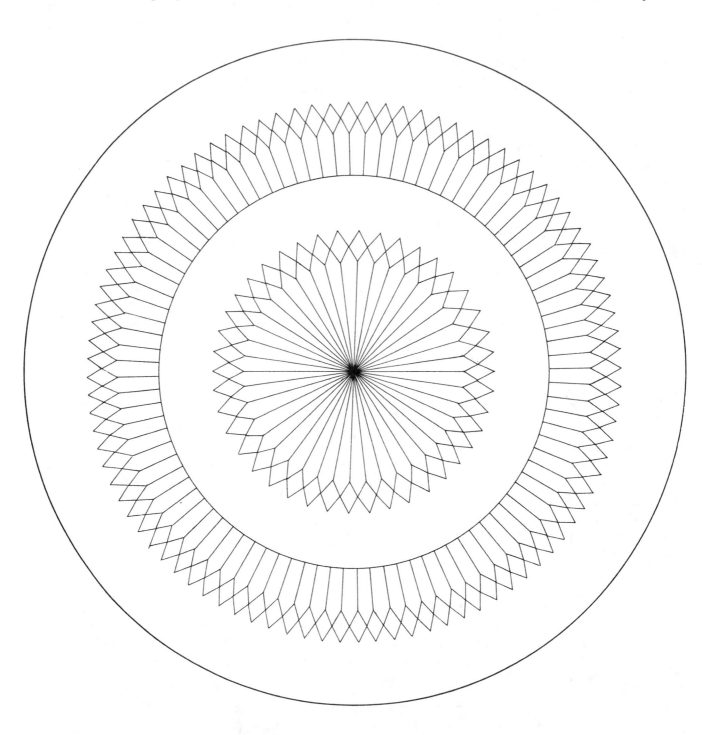

Colors found to date:

- Amethyst (odd pieces)
- Pink
- Crystal*
- White (odd pieces)
- Iridescent

*Crystal may be found with a gold or silver rim.

# ANNIVERSARY

**Reproductions or reissues**

None are known.

**General pattern notes**

Strictly speaking, the 1947-49 date is inaccurate. Jeanette began producing the pattern in pink only in those years, but it made Anniversary in the crystal and iridescent right up into the 1970s. Most collectors do not seriously consider these two colors part of Depression glass collecting. The value listing below contains only those items that were in the 1947 pattern produced in pink.

| ITEM & DESCRIPTION | DOLLAR VALUE RANGES BY COLOR |
| --- | --- |
| | Pink |
| Bowl, 4-7/8" | 8-10 |
| Bowl, 7-3/8" | 16-18 |
| Bowl, 9" | 24-26 |
| Butter dish and cover | 60-70 |
| Candy jar and cover | 45-50 |
| Compote (three legged) | 12-15 |
| Cake plate, 12-1/2" | 16-18 |
| Creamer (footed) | 10-12 |
| Cup | 8-10 |
| Pickle dish, 9" | 12-15 |
| Plate, 6-1/4" | 4-5 |
| Plate, 9" | 15-18 |
| Plate, 12-1/2" | 12-15 |
| Relish dish, 8" | 12-15 |
| Saucer | 3-5 |
| Sherbet (footed) | 8-10 |
| Sugar and cover | 35-40 |
| Vase, 6-1/2" | 35-40 |
| Wall vase | 50-60 |
| Wine glass | 14-16 |

# AUNT POLLY

c. 1920

U. S. Glass Company

*Pittsburgh, Pennsylvania

**Colors found to date:**

- Blue
- Green
- Iridescent (amber)

\* The company had numerous locations for factories.  Pittsburgh was one of the only two factories still operating in 1938.

# AUNT POLLY

**Reproduction or reissues**

None found to date.

**General pattern notes**

For many years, the manufacturer of this pattern was not known, but recently, catalog evidence was found that identifies the U.S. Glass Company as its maker.

Rarest of the pattern are the salt and pepper shakers, oval bowls, and sugars with a cover.

| ITEM & DESCRIPTION | DOLLAR VALUE RANGES BY COLOR | |
|---|---|---|
| | **Blue** | **Green & Iridescent** |
| Bowl, 4-3/8" | 16-18 | 12-14 |
| Bowl, 4-3/4" | 20-30 | 24-26 |
| Bowl, 7-1/4" (oval, handled) | 35-40 | 30-35 |
| Bowl, 7-7/8" | 45-50 | 35-40 |
| Bowl, 8-3/8" (oval) | 100-125 | 85-95 |
| Butter dish and cover | 225-245 | 195-210 |
| Creamer | 45-50 | 35-40 |
| Pitcher, 8" | 175-200 | — |
| Plate, 6" | 10-12 | 8-10 |
| Plate, 8" | 18-20 | — |
| Salt and pepper shakers (pair) | 225-245 | — |
| Sherbet | 12-14 | 8-10 |
| Sugar and cover | 175-195 | 85-95 |
| Tumbler, 8 oz. | 30-35 | — |
| Vase, 6-1/2" (footed) | 45-50 | 35-40 |

# AVOCADO

### 1923 - 1933

Indiana Glass Company                                    Dunkirk, Indiana

**Colors found to date:**

- Crystal        • Green        • Pink        • White

# AVOCADO

## Reproductions or reissues

Back in the early- to mid-1970s, Indiana Glass introduced what it described as a reissue (taken from the original molds) of the Avocado pattern in tumblers and a pitcher in pink, red, frosted pink, green, a dark blue or purple color, and amber. The only one to worry about presently is the pink. That is the only duplication of the original colors in the pattern. The reissued pink appears to have an orange cast to the color so you should be able to easily identify the new pieces if you can compare them to the old pink color. These new pieces are distributed exclusively through a home party plan by a company named Tiara.

## General pattern notes

The company calls this its "No. 601 Line" and the name Avocado was given it by collectors. Curiously, early company advertisements refer to it as a pear and bead design. The fruits do resemble avocados, however, and that is what collectors call it. Apparently, the company has acquiesced to this with the new issues.

The most difficult to find of the items in this pattern are the pitchers and tumblers in green and most of the saucers.

The whole Avocado pattern line is generally hard to find.

| ITEM & DESCRIPTION | DOLLAR VALUE RANGES BY COLOR | |
| --- | --- | --- |
| | Green | Pink |
| Bowl, 5-1/4" (two-handled) | 35-40 | 30-35 |
| Bowl, 6" (footed) | 35-40 | 30-35 |
| Bowl, 7" (one-handled) | 38-42 | 35-38 |
| Bowl, 7-1/2" | 48-52 | 40-45 |
| Bowl, 8" (two-handled, oval) | 45-50 | 40-45 |
| Bowl, 8-1/2" | 50-55 | 45-50 |
| Bowl, 9-1/2" | 150-175 | 100-125 |
| Creamer (footed) | 32-34 | 30-32 |
| Cup (footed) | 34-36 | 30-32 |
| Pitcher | 1,200-1,300 | 325-350 |
| Plate, 6-1/4" | 18-24 | 8-10 |
| Plate, 8-1/4" | 22-24 | 12-14 |
| Plate, 10-1/4" (cake) | 60-70 | 50-55 |
| Saucer | 20-22 | 16-18 |
| Sherbet | 50-60 | 45-50 |
| Sugar (footed) | 32-34 | 25-30 |
| Tumbler | 300-320 | 250-275 |

# BEADED BLOCK

## c. 1930

Imperial Glass Company

Bellaire, Ohio

Drawing above is of a cross-section showing the high relief of this pattern.

Colors found to date:

- Amber
- Iridescent*
- Blue
- Opalescent
- Crystal
- Pink
- Green
- Vaseline

\* Still being manufactured in pink.

# BEADED BLOCK

**Reproductions or reissues**
    None found to date.

**General pattern notes**
    This pattern has a good heavy quality feel to it. You would almost believe it to be a much higher quality glass than that normally associated with Depression glass. Some items are still being produced today and manufactured in pink. One easy way to identify newer pieces is to look for a small "IG" mold embossed on the plate. The company began adding this trademark in February of 1951.

| ITEM & DESCRIPTION | DOLLAR VALUE RANGES BY COLOR | | | |
| --- | --- | --- | --- | --- |
| | Amber | Crystal | Green/Pink | Other colors |
| Bowl, 4-1/2" (two-handled) | 18-20 | 6-8 | 24-26 | 28-30 |
| Bowl, 4-1/2" (round lily) | 16-18 | 8 10 | 22-24 | 26-28 |
| Bowl, 5-1/2" (square) | 18-20 | 8-10 | 22-26 | 28-30 |
| Bowl, 5-1/2" (one handle) | 18-20 | 8-10 | 24-26 | 28-30 |
| Bowl, 6" (round) | 22-24 | 8-10 | 28-28 | 30-32 |
| Bowl, 6-1/4" (round) | 22-24 | 10-12 | 26-28 | 30-32 |
| Bowl, 6-1/2 (round) | 22-24 | 10-12 | 26-28 | 30-32 |
| Bowl, 6-1/2" (two-handled) | 26-28 | 12-14 | 30-32 | 32-36 |
| Bowl, 6-3/4" (round) | 22-24 | 10-12 | 32-34 | 28-30 |
| Bowl, 7-1/4" (round) | 26-28 | 14-16 | 30-32 | 32-34 |
| Bowl, 7-1/2" (round, fluted edge) | 26-28 | 14-16 | 30-32 | 32-34 |
| Bowl, 7-1/2" (round) | 26-28 | 10-12 | 30-32 | 32-34 |
| Bowl, 8-1/4" (celery) | 28-32 | 10-12 | 32-34 | 36-40 |
| Creamer | 18-20 | 10-12 | 20-22 | 24-26 |
| Pitcher, 5-1/4" | 100-125 | 50-65 | 145-165 | 165-185 |
| Plate, 7-3/4" (square) | 18-20 | 6-8 | 20-22 | 24-26 |
| Plate, 8-3/4" | 22-24 | 6-8 | 26-28 | 30-32 |
| Stemmed jelly, 4-1/2" | 30-35 | 8-10 | 34-38 | 38-40 |
| Stemmed jelly, 4-1/2" (flared lid) | 35-40 | 12-14 | 38-40 | 40-45 |
| Sugar | 18-20 | 10-16 | 22-24 | 24-26 |
| Vase, 6" | 22-24 | 10-12 | 26-28 | 30-32 |

# BLOCK OPTIC
### 1929 - 1933

Hocking Glass Company                    (now Anchor-Hocking Glass Corporation)

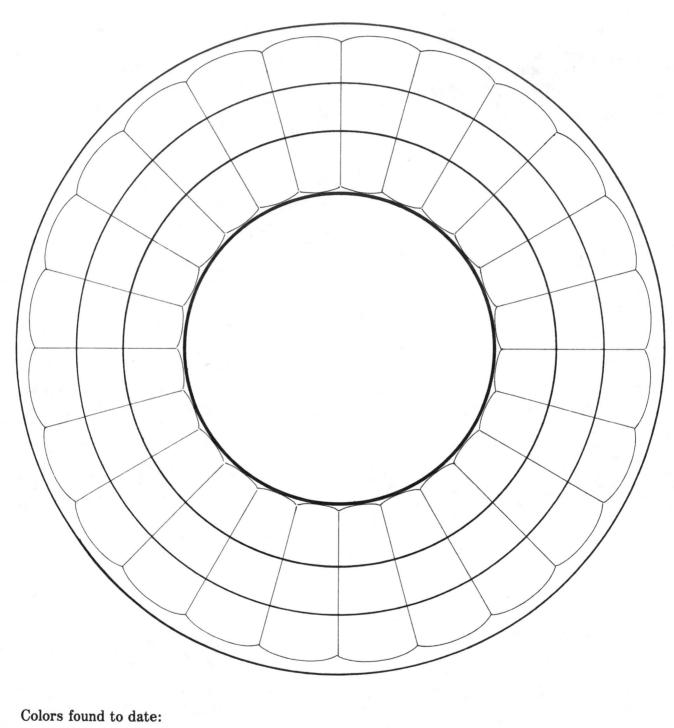

Colors found to date:

- Crystal        • Green        • Pink        • Yellow

# BLOCK OPTIC

## Reproductions or reissues
None found to date.

## General pattern notes
Sometimes known simply as "Block," Block Optic is heard more often today.

Green was the color produced most and yellow is difficult to uncover in any quantity. There were a small amount of pieces produced in a satin or frosty finish. It may be that only the sugar and creamer were made with the satin finish, but keep your eyes open. The items with black stems and/or bases are quite elusive. Other scarce pieces are the odd items such as candlesticks, vases, mugs, etc.

You might also note that there is no round butter dish to be found in Block Optic. All that have ever turned up are rectangular. Some dinner plates have a snowflake design in the center.

| ITEM & DESCRIPTION | DOLLAR VALUE RANGES BY COLOR | | |
| --- | --- | --- | --- |
| | Green | Pink | Yellow |
| Bowl, 4-1/4" | 8-10 | 10-12 | — |
| Bowl, 5-1/4" | 15-18 | 25-30 | — |
| Bowl, 7" | 126-145 | 145-165 | 125-145 |
| Bowl, 8-1/2" | 26-28 | 30-35 | — |
| Butter dish and cover | 50-60 | — | — |
| Candlesticks, 1-3/4", pr | 110-125 | 95-100 | — |
| Candy jar and cover | 60-65 | 65-70 | 60-65 |
| Compote, 4" | 35-40 | 80-85 | — |
| Creamers (five styles) | 12-14 | 14-16 | 12-14 |
| Cups (four styles) | 6-8 | 4-7 | 6-8 |
| Goblet, 4" | 35-40 | 35-40 | — |
| Goblet, 4-1/2" | 40-45 | 40-45 | — |
| Goblet, 5-3/4" | 28-30 | 28-30 | — |
| Goblet, 7-1/4" | — | — | 35-40 |
| Ice bucket | 45-50 | 65-75 | — |
| Ice or butter tub | 75-80 | 95-100 | — |
| Mug | 45-50 | — | — |
| Pitcher, 7-5/8" | 75-85 | 100-125 | — |
| Pitcher, 8" | 95-110 | 110-135 | — |
| Pitcher, 8-1/2" | 65-70 | 65-70 | — |
| Plate, 6" | 3-4 | 5-6 | 5-6 |
| Plate, 8-1/4" | 5-7 | 6-8 | 6-8 |
| Plate, 9" | 25-30 | 35-40 | 35-40 |
| Plate, 9" (grill) | 65-70 | 70-75 | — |
| Plate, 10-1/4" | 24-26 | 28-30 | — |
| Salt and pepper (footed), pair | 75-85 | 100-125 | 145-165 |
| Salt and pepper | 125-135 | — | — |
| Sandwich server (center-handled) | 65-75 | 75-80 | — |
| Saucer, 5-3/4" | 6-8 | 6-8 | — |
| Saucer, 6-1/8" | 6-8 | 6-8 | 11-14 |
| Sherbet (cone shape) | 8-10 | — | — |
| Sherbet, 3-1/4" | 6-8 | 8-10 | 6-8 |
| Sherbet, 4-3/4" | 16-18 | 18-20 | 20-22 |

| ITEM & DESCRIPTION | DOLLAR VALUE RANGES BY COLOR | | |
|---|---|---|---|
| | Green | Pink | Yellow |
| Sugar (three styles) | 12-14 | 18-20 | 12-14 |
| Tumbler, 3-1/2" | 20-24 | 24-26 | — |
| Tumbler, 4" (footed) | 16-18 | 18-20 | — |
| Tumbler, 9 oz. | 20-22 | 22-24 | — |
| Tumbler, 9 oz. (footed) | 22-24 | 24-26 | 18-22 |
| Tumbler, 10 oz. | 24-26 | 24-26 | — |
| Tumbler, 6", 10 oz. (footed) | 26-28 | 28-30 | 28-30 |
| "Tumble-up Night Set" (3" tumbler and bottle) | 75-85 | — | — |
| Vase, 5-3/4" | 250-275 | — | — |
| Whiskey jigger, 2-1/2" | 35-38 | 38-40 | — |

# BOWKNOT

c. 1930
Manufacturer Unknown

**Colors found to date:**

- Crystal (rare)
- Green

# BOWKNOT

**Reproductions or reissues**

None found to date.

**General pattern notes**

Little can be said about this pattern named Bowknot by collectors until some evidence surfaces as to the manufacturer. It appears always in green, but there has been an unsubstantiated report of it being in crystal.

The listing of eight pieces below indicates a saucer because of the known cups. As yet, no saucers have turned up.

| ITEM & DESCRIPTION | DOLLAR VALUE RANGES BY COLOR |
| --- | --- |
| | Green |
| Bowl, 4-1/2" | 18-20 |
| Bowl, 5-1/2" | 28-30 |
| Cup | 9-12 |
| Plate, 7" | 12-14 |
| Sherbet (footed) | 16-18 |
| Tumbler, 5" | 24-28 |
| Tumbler, 5" (footed) | 22-24 |

# BUBBLE

(see  General Pattern Notes for dates)

Hocking Glass Corporation                                    (now Anchor Hocking Glass Corporation)

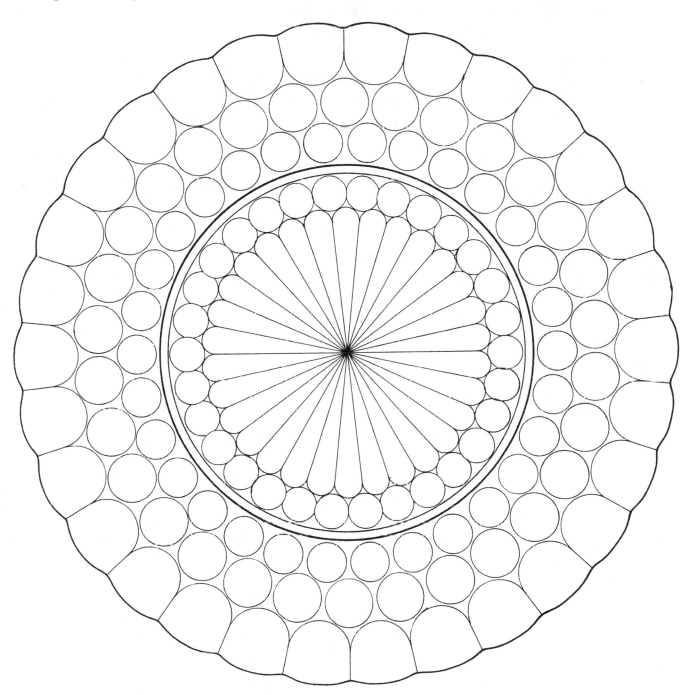

Colors to be found:

- Blue (pale)        • Crystal          • Green (dark)
- Pink               • Ruby Red         • White (milk white)

# BUBBLE

### Reproductions or reissues

None found to date.

### General pattern notes

Bubble has been variously known as "Bullseye" and "Provincial" in the past, due to the company issuing the pattern under those names as well. The names referred to new color issues in the pattern and make it fairly easy to date most of the items.

The green ("Forest Green") and the crystal were issued in 1937; the Ruby Red was issued later in 1963; the pale or light blue was first issued in 1937.

Some of the more rare pieces are the creamer in blue and any flanged bowl.

| ITEM & DESCRIPTION | DOLLAR VALUE RANGES BY COLOR | | | |
|---|---|---|---|---|
| | Blue | Green | Red | Crystal |
| Bowl, 4" | 18-20 | 16-18 | — | 2-6 |
| Bowl, 4-1/2" | 12-14 | 14-16 | 12-14 | 2-6 |
| Bowl, 5-1/4" | 12-14 | 14-16 | 12-14 | 3-8 |
| Bowl, 7-3/4" | 20-24 | 28-30 | — | 8-10 |
| Bowl, 8-3/8" | 26-28 | 28-30 | 26-28 | 8-10 |
| Bowl, 9" (flanged) | 65-75 | — | — | — |
| Candlesticks | — | 45-60 | — | 15-21 |
| Creamer | 28-30 | 15-18 | — | 6-8 |
| Cup | 4-6 | 8-10 | 8-10 | 2-6 |
| Lamp | — | — | — | 35-40 |
| Pitcher | — | — | 60-65 | 38-47 |
| Plate, 6-3/4" | 3-6 | 2-5 | — | 2-5 |
| Plate, 9-3/8" (grill) | 25-30 | — | — | — |
| Plate, 9-3/8" | 10-12 | 35-38 | 32-35 | 5-6 |
| Platter, 12" (oval) | 20-22 | — | — | 10-12 |
| Saucer | 2-4 | 3-4 | 3-4 | 1-2 |
| Sugar | — | 6-9 | — | 6-8 |
| Tidbit (two-level) | — | — | 45-50 | — |
| Tumbler, 6 oz. | — | — | 10-12 | 3-7 |
| Tumbler, 9 oz. | — | — | 12-14 | 8-10 |
| Tumbler, 12 oz. | — | — | 12-14 | — |
| Tumbler, 16 oz. | — | — | 18-20 | — |
| Tumbler, 16 oz. (footed) | — | — | — | 12-14 |

# CAMEO

## 1930 - 1934

Hocking Glass Company                    (now Anchor Hocking Glass Corporation)

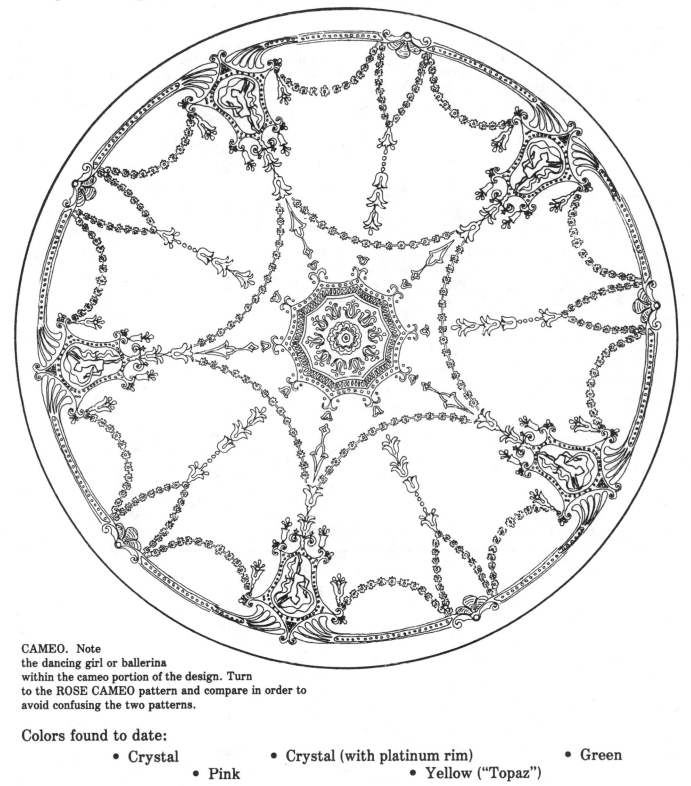

CAMEO. Note
the dancing girl or ballerina
within the cameo portion of the design. Turn
to the ROSE CAMEO pattern and compare in order to
avoid confusing the two patterns.

## Colors found to date:

- Crystal
- Pink
- Crystal (with platinum rim)
- Yellow ("Topaz")
- Green

# CAMEO

## Reproductions or reissues

The salt and pepper shakers were reported in pink. This writer has not seen them, but dealers have spoken of them as having a light or faint pattern when compared to the genuine pieces. They appeared in 1982. There is a modern addition to the pattern. Found in pink, green, or gold, they are child-size pieces, tumblers, ice bucket, a footed bowl, plates, cups, saucers, creamers, sugars, butter dishes, and candle holders. They are technically not reproductions, for they were never produced as part of the original line.

## General pattern notes

Cameo (also known as "Ballerina" and "Dancing Girl") is one of the most popularly collected Depression-glass patterns. It is also widely available due to the enormous number of pieces manufactured. Some, however, are extremely rare and valuable (note the prices in the listing). The rarest of all is, of course, the center-handled sandwich server, but then, so are all the center-ringed or cup-ringed saucers. Unless you own a gold mine, give up the idea of a complete set—but you can still gather a useful set of basic pieces for a reasonable outlay.

| ITEM & DESCRIPTION | DOLLAR VALUE RANGES BY COLOR | | | |
| --- | --- | --- | --- | --- |
| | Crystal | Green | Pink | Yellow (Topaz) |
| Bowl, 4-1/4" | 4-5 | — | — | — |
| Bowl, 4-3/4" (cream soup) | — | 135-145 | — | — |
| Bowl, 5-1/2" | 5-6 | 28-30 | — | 28-30 |
| Bowl, 7-1/4" | — | 50-60 | — | — |
| Bowl, 8-1/4" | — | 45-50 | 125-145 | — |
| Bowl, 9" (rimmed) | — | 85-95 | — | — |
| Bowl, 10" (oval) | — | 38-40 | — | 32-38 |
| Bowl, 11" (console, three-legged) | — | 75-85 | 60-70 | 95-110 |
| Butter dish (covered) | — | 225-250 | — | 1,000-1,200 |
| Cake plate, 10" (three-legged) | — | 35-40 | — | — |
| Cake plate, 10-1/2" | — | 100-125 | — | — |
| Candlesticks, 4" (pair) | — | 120-135 | — | — |
| Candy jar, 4" (covered) | — | 95-100 | 475-495 | 100-125 |
| Candy jar, 6-1/2" (covered) | — | 175-195 | — | — |
| Cocktail shaker (metal lid) | 750-850 | — | — | — |
| Compote, 5" | — | 50-60 | — | — |
| Cookie jar with cover | — | 65-75 | — | — |
| Creamer, 3-1/4" | — | 20-24 | — | 24-28 |
| Creamer, 4-1/4" | — | 24-26 | 95-100 | — |
| Cup (two styles) | — | 14-16 | 85-95 | 8-10 |
| Decanter, 10" (with stopper) | — | 185-200 | — | — |
| Decanter, 10" (with stopper, frosted) | — | 45-50 | — | — |
| Domino tray, 7" (3" ring) | — | 165-175 | — | — |
| Domino tray, 7" (no ring) | 125-145 | — | 250-295 | — |
| Goblet, 3-1/2" | — | 850-900 | 850-950 | — |
| Goblet, 4" | — | 80-90 | 225-245 | — |
| Goblet, 6" | — | 55-65 | 175-200 | — |
| Ice bowl, 3" x 5-1/2" | 245-295 | 185-200 | 650-700 | — |
| Jar, 2" (covered) | 150-165 | 175-200 | — | — |
| *Pitcher, 5-3/4" | — | 250-295 | — | 1,200-1,400 |
| *Pitcher, 6" | — | 75-85 | — | — |

| ITEM & DESCRIPTION | DOLLAR VALUE RANGES BY COLOR | | | |
|---|---|---|---|---|
| | Crystal | Green | Pink | Yellow (Topaz) |
| Pitcher, 8-1/2" | 375-395 | 75-85 | — | — |
| (Some pitchers have a rope design ringing the pitcher just below the top) | | | | |
| Plate, 6" | 3-4 | 5-6 | 65-75 | 3-6 |
| Plate, 7" | 4-5 | — | — | — |
| Plate, 8" | 6-8 | 12-14 | 35-40 | 10-12 |
| Plate, 8-1/2" (square) | — | 65-75 | — | 175-200 |
| Plate, 9-1/2" | — | 24-26 | 65-75 | 12-14 |
| Plate, 10" | — | 20-22 | 60-65 | — |
| Plate, 10-1/2" (grill) | — | 12-14 | 50-60 | 18-20 |
| Plate, 10-1/2" (grill, closed handles) | — | 65-75 | — | 10-12 |
| Plate, 11-1/2" (closed handles) | — | 14-16 | — | 12-14 |
| Platter, 12" (closed handles) | — | 28-30 | — | 35-40 |
| Relish, 7-1/2" | | | | |
| (footed, three sections) | 125-145 | 30-35 | — | — |
| Salt and pepper (pair, footed) | — | 95-100 | 750-850* | — |
| Sandwich server (centered handle) | — | 4,500-5,000 | — | — |
| Saucer (cup ringed) | — | 125-145 | — | — |
| Saucer, 6" (same as sherbet, plate) | — | 5-6 | 65-75 | 3-6 |
| Sherbet, 3-1/8" | — | 18-20 | 65-75 | 35-40 |
| Sherbet, 4-7/8" | — | 35-40 | 95-100 | 45-50 |
| Sugar, 3-1/4" | — | 20-24 | — | 15-21 |
| Sugar, 4-1/4" | — | 24-26 | 95-100 | — |
| Tumbler, 3-3/4" | — | 40-45 | 85-95 | — |
| Tumbler, 4" | 12-15 | 35-40 | 75-80 | — |
| Tumbler, 4-3/4" | — | 35-40 | — | — |
| Tumbler, 5" | — | 45-50 | 100-125 | 50-60 |
| Tumbler, 5-1/4" | — | 75-85 | — | — |
| Tumbler, 3 oz. (footed) | — | 65-75 | 115-125 | 50-60 |
| Tumbler, 5", 9 oz. (footed) | — | 30-35 | 115-125 | 20-24 |
| Tumbler, 5-3/4" (footed) | — | 65-75 | — | — |
| Tumbler, 6-3/8", 15 oz., ftd | — | 500-550 | — | — |
| Vase, 5-3/4" | — | 245-265 | — | — |
| Vase, 8" | — | 50-60 | — | — |
| Water bottle (Whitehouse vinegar) | — | 20-25 | — | — |
| *Still being manufactured in pink, this value is for the older, original pair. | | | | |

# CHERRYBERRY
# C. 1930
### (See STRAWBERRY, Page 199)

# CHERRY BLOSSOM

### 1930 s

Jeannette Glass Company

Jeannette, Pennsylvania

**Colors found to date:**

- Crystal (odd pieces)
- Jadite (opaque green)
- Delphite (opaque blue)
- Pink
- Green
- Red

# CHERRY BLOSSOM

## Reproductions or reissues

Many pieces of Cherry Blossom have been reproduced and available from the A.A. Importing Co., Inc. The following is a listing of those pieces that are on the market, all in pink, green, or red.

Butter dish (covered)           Dinner plate (9")
Pitcher (6-3/4")                 Cup and saucer
Tumblers (4-3/8", footed)        Butter dish (red)
Salad plate (6")                 Pitcher (red)
Bowl (6")                        Tumbler (red)
Bowl (8-3/8")                    Tray (12")
Salt and pepper shakers (delphite—this color never made in original line salt and peppers)

The major identifying differences between the old and the new follows:

Pitchers—old have nine cherries on the underside of the base. The new ones have only seven.

Tumblers—old have either two or three separate, close rings around the edge, just below the lip. The new tumblers have only one single ring there.

Shakers (a few of the reproduction shakers were dated "77" on the base, but not all)—the easiest way to tell new from old is the amount of solid glass in the bottom inside down at the base. The new ones have more than twice as much solid glass than the old.

Butter dishes—the flange pattern on the old ones extends right out to the edge of the rim and on the new ones, the pattern stops short of the rim.

The overall pattern quality on all these pieces is definitely lower than the originals.

Another reproduction of unknown source is that of the child's set. The original set was called "Jeannette's Junior Dinner Set" and consisted of four each of 6" plates, cups and saucers, a creamer, and an uncovered sugar bowl for a total of 14 pieces. They are scaled down to about one-third of the regular tableware size and were available in pink and delphite.

The reproductions are of decidedly lower quality in color, pattern, and overall appearance. Some of them even have upside-down designs. The reproductions are of a cup, saucer, and, for some unknown reason, a butter dish. The cup and saucer appear in pink and delphite; the butter dish was made in cobalt blue. No problem there, for the original butter dish was never made in that color. The cups and saucers are crude copies at best.

## General pattern notes

Cherry Blossom is also a popular, heavily collected pattern in Depression glass.

Some significant variations are due to design changes over the years. For instance, in the first years of production, all footed pieces sported round bases. They were later given scalloped bases, but not exclusively. The best way to identify a newer one is by its shape. The earlier pitchers were cone-shaped, while the newer ones were more rounded.

The delphite color didn't appear until about 1936.

All the salt and pepper shakers are quite rare and hard to find.

The patterns are also known to appear all over an item or on the top only.

Salt and pepper shakers appear in pink and green only.

| ITEM & DESCRIPTION | DOLLAR VALUE RANGES BY COLOR | | | |
|---|---|---|---|---|
| | Delphite | Green | Jadeite | Pink |
| Bowl, 4-3/4" | 16-18 | 18-20 | — | 20-22 |
| Bowl, 5-3/4" | — | 45-50 | — | 50-60 |
| Bowl, 7-3/4" | — | 90-95 | — | 90-95 |
| Bowl, 8-1/2" | 55-65 | 50-55 | — | 50-55 |
| Bowl, 9" (oval) | 55-65 | 50-55 | — | 55-60 |
| Bowl, 9" (two handled) | 35-45 | 60-65 | — | 50-55 |
| Bowl, 10-1/2" (three-legged) | — | 95-100 | 325-350 | 95-100 |
| Butter dish and cover | — | 100-125 | — | 95-100 |
| Cake tray, 10-1/4" (three-legged) | — | 40-45 | — | 35-40 |
| Coaster | — | 16-18 | — | 20-22 |
| Cookie jar | — | — | — | 8,000-10,000 |
| Creamer | 20-22 | 20-22 | — | 20-24 |
| Cup | 22-24 | 20-22 | — | 20-22 |
| Mug | — | 250-300 | — | 300-350 |

| ITEM & DESCRIPTION | DOLLAR VALUE RANGES BY COLOR | | | |
|---|---|---|---|---|
| | Delphite | Green | Jadeite | Pink |
| Pitcher, 6-3/4" | 95-100 | 60-65 | — | 55-65 |
| Pitcher, 7" | — | 75-80 | — | 75-80 |
| Pitcher, 8" (footed) | — | 65-75 | — | 75-85 |
| Plate, 6" | 12-14 | 7-9 | — | 5-8 |
| Plate, 7" | — | 25-30 | — | 25-30 |
| Plate, 9" | 15-18 | 28-30 | 40-50 | 25-30 |
| Plate, 9" (grill) | — | 30-35 | | 35-38 |
| Plate, 10" (grill) | — | 100-125 | — | — |
| Platter, 9" (oval) | — | 1,100-1,200 | — | 1,500-1,800 |
| Platter, 11" (oval) | 40-50 | 50-60 | — | 50-60 |
| Platter, 13" (also 13" sectioned) | — | 85-95 | — | 85-95 |
| Salt and pepper | — | 900-1,000 | — | 1,400-1,600 |
| Saucer | 4-5 | 6-7 | — | 5-7 |
| Sherbet | 14-16 | 20-22 | — | 18-20 |
| Sugar and cover | 15-18 | 40-45 | — | 35-38 |
| Tray (sandwich, 10-1/2") | 28-30 | 45-48 | — | 40-45 |
| Tumbler, 3-3/4" (footed) | 22-27 | 35-40 | — | 30-35 |
| Tumbler, 4-1/2", 9 oz. (footed) | 22-24 | 40-45 | — | 35-40 |
| Tumbler, 4-1/2", 8 oz. (footed) | 22-24 | 40-45 | — | 35-40 |
| Tumbler, 3-1/2" | — | 24-28 | — | 20-22 |
| Tumbler, 4-1/4" | — | 24-26 | — | 18-20 |
| Tumbler, 5" | — | 95-100 | — | 85-95 |
| **JEANNETTE'S JUNIOR DINNER SET (Pink or Delphite)** | | | | |
| Creamer | 45-50 | | | |
| Cup | 45-50 | | | |
| Plate | 15-18 | | | |
| Saucer | 10-12 | | | |
| Sugar | 45-50 | | | |
| Entire 14-piece set | 375-400 | | | |
| Original box adds about $45 to the price. | | | | |

# CIRCLE

Hocking Glass Company                    (now Anchor-Hocking Glass Corporation)

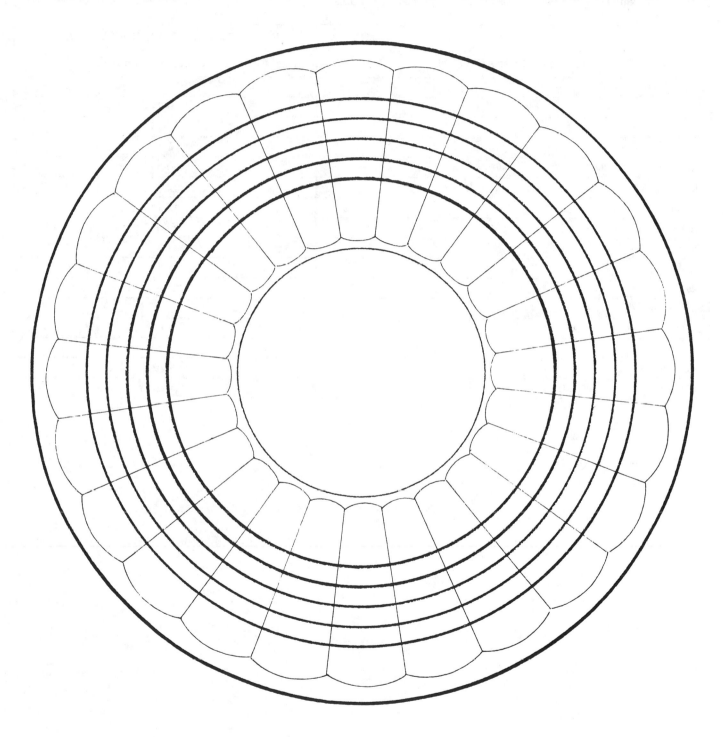

Colors found to date:

- Crystal          • Green          • Pink

# CIRCLE

**Reproductions or reissues**

None known to date.

**General pattern notes**

At present, the green color is most commonly found. Some pink is found and so far, the crystal exists only as a catalog listing. Some pieces in the pattern have center-ray designs, but in some they are absent. So far, the larger pieces seem to be hardest to find.

| ITEM & DESCRIPTION | DOLLAR VALUE RANGES BY COLOR |
| --- | --- |
| | **Green or Pink** |
| Bowl, 4-1/2" | 8-10 |
| Bowl, 8" | 20-24 |
| Creamer | 12-15 |
| Cup (two styles) | 6-8 |
| Decanter (with handle) | 60-65 |
| Goblet, 4-1/2" | 12-15 |
| Goblet, 8 oz. | 12-15 |
| Pitcher | 50-60 |
| Plate, 6" | 4-5 |
| Plate, 9-1/2" | 15-18 |
| Saucer | 3-4 |
| Sherbet, 3-1/8" | 6-8 |
| Sherbet, 4-3/4" | 8-10 |
| Sugar | 12-15 |
| Tumbler, 4 oz. | 8-10 |
| Tumbler, 8 oz. | 10-12 |

# CLOVERLEAF

## 1931 - 1936

Hazel Atlas Glass Company

Clarksburg, West Virginia and Zanesville, Ohio

Colors found to date:

- Black
- Crystal
- Green
- Pink
- Yellow

# CLOVERLEAF

**Reproductions or reissues**
None known to date.

**General pattern notes**
Cloverleaf is tough to find in any quantity most of the time, with black being the most elusive of all the colors. It was a small line with only 19 different items offered, based upon what has been uncovered so far. Only 10 of these have been found in black.

| ITEM & DESCRIPTION | DOLLAR VALUE RANGES BY COLOR | | | |
|---|---|---|---|---|
| | **Black** | **Green** | **Pink** | **Yellow** |
| Ashtray, 4" | 60-65 | — | — | — |
| Ashtray, 5-3/4" | 85-95 | — | — | — |
| Bowl, 4" | — | 25-30 | 20-24 | 24-28 |
| Bowl, 5" | — | 50-60 | — | 45-50 |
| Bowl, 7" | — | 45-50 | — | 40-50 |
| Bowl, 8" | — | 75-85 | — | — |
| Candy dish and cover | — | 75-85 | — | 110-125 |
| Creamer (footed) | 18-20 | 12-15 | — | 20-24 |
| Cup | 18-20 | 12-15 | 8-10 | 20-24 |
| Plate, 6" | 35-40 | 8-10 | — | 8-10 |
| Plate, 8" | 18-20 | 12-15 | 14-16 | 16-18 |
| Plate, 10-1/4" (grill) | — | 30-35 | — | 28-30 |
| Salt and pepper shakers (shaker, pair) | 95-100 | 65-75 | — | 100-125 |
| Saucer | 6-8 | 8-10 | 4-5 | 4-5 |
| Sherbet (footed) | 20-24 | 10-12 | 6-8 | 8-10 |
| Sugar, 3-5/8" (footed) | 18-20 | 12-15 | — | 20-24 |
| Tumbler, 4" | — | 50-55 | — | — |
| Tumbler, 3-3/4" (flared base) | — | 55-60 | — | — |
| Tumbler, 5-3/4" (footed) | — | 30-35 | — | 28-30 |

# COLONIAL
### 1934 - 1938

Hocking Glass Company                    (now Anchor-Hocking Glass Corporation)

**Colors found to date:**

- Crystal          • Green          • Pink

# COLONIAL

## Reproductions or reissues
None known to exist.

## General pattern notes
Colonial is a pattern taken from an elegant, classic old pressed-glass design known as "Knife and Fork," hence the commonly used alternate name for the pattern.

The pattern is relatively hard to collect, as there aren't too many pieces available today.

An unusual item to be found in Depression glass patterns is the "spooner" (spoon or celery holder), but it is found in this pattern.

There seems to be an unusually large number of tumbler styles to choose from, though none but the smallest sizes are in anything close to plentiful supply. Mugs are quite rare in any of the colors, but a green one would be an exceedingly fine prize.

| ITEMS & DESCRIPTION | DOLLAR VALUE RANGES BY COLOR | | |
| --- | --- | --- | --- |
| | Crystal | Green | Pink |
| Bowl, 3-3/4" | — | — | 50-55 |
| Bowl, 4-1/2" | 8-10 | 18-20 | 18-20 |
| Bowl, 5-1/2" | 18-20 | 85-95 | 65-75 |
| Bowl, 4-1/2" (cream soup) | 40-45 | 65-75 | 65-75 |
| Bowl, 7" | 20-24 | 65-70 | 65-70 |
| Bowl, 9" | 20-24 | 30-35 | 30-35 |
| Bowl, 10" (oval) | 20-24 | 35-40 | 35-40 |
| Butter dish and cover | 35-40 | 60-65 | 650-700 |
| Cheese dish | — | 225-240 | — |
| Creamer, 5" | 16-18 | 30-35 | 45-50 |
| Cup | 6-8 | 16-18 | 16-18 |
| Cordial, 3-3/4" | 14-16 | 28-30 | — |
| Goblet, 4" | 8-10 | 24-28 | — |
| Goblet, 4-1/2" | 8-10 | 28-30 | — |
| Goblet, 5-1/4" | 8-10 | 24-28 | — |
| Goblet, 5-3/4" | 10-12 | 30-35 | — |
| Mug, 4-1/2" | — | 700-800 | 450-500 |
| Pitcher, 7" | 28-30 | 60-65 | 60-65 |
| Pitcher, 7-3/4" | 30-35 | 75-80 | 75-80 |
| Pitcher (pink with beaded top) | — | — | 1,000-1,200 |
| Plate, 6" | 3-5 | 6-8 | 6-8 |
| Plate, 8-1/2" | 6-8 | 10-12 | 10-12 |
| Plate, 10" | 20-24 | 65-70 | 60-65 |
| Plate, 10" (grill) | 14-16 | 24-26 | 26-28 |
| Platter, 12" (oval) | 16-18 | 30-35 | 35-40 |
| Salt and pepper (shaker, pair) | 50-60 | 145-160 | 145-160 |
| Saucer | 3-5 | 6-8 | 6-8 |
| Sherbet, 3" | — | — | 20-24 |
| Sherbet, 3-3/8" | 6-8 | 14-16 | 12-14 |
| Spoon or celery holder (two-handled) | 45-60 | 125-135 | 125-135 |
| Sugar and cover, 6" | 20-24 | 45-50 | 65-75 |
| Tumbler, 3" | 8-10 | 24-26 | 18-20 |
| Tumbler, 4" | 8-10 | 24-26 | 24-26 |

| ITEMS & DESCRIPTION | DOLLAR VALUE RANGES BY COLOR | | |
|---|---|---|---|
| | Crystal | Green | Pink |
| Tumbler, 10 oz. | 16-18 | 20-24 | 20-24 |
| Tumbler, 12 oz. | 16-18 | 50-55 | 50-55 |
| Tumbler, 15 oz. | 30-35 | 65-75 | 60-65 |
| Tumbler, 3-1/4" (footed) | 8-10 | 24-26 | 22-24 |
| Tumbler, 4", 5 oz. (footed) | 12-14 | 40-45 | 35-40 |
| Tumbler, 5-1/4" (footed) | 16-18 | 40-45 | 40-45 |
| Whiskey jigger, 2-1/2" | 10-12 | 18-20 | |

# COLONIAL BLOCK

## 1930 s

Hazel Atlas Glass Company                    Clarksburg, West Virginia and Zanesville, Ohio

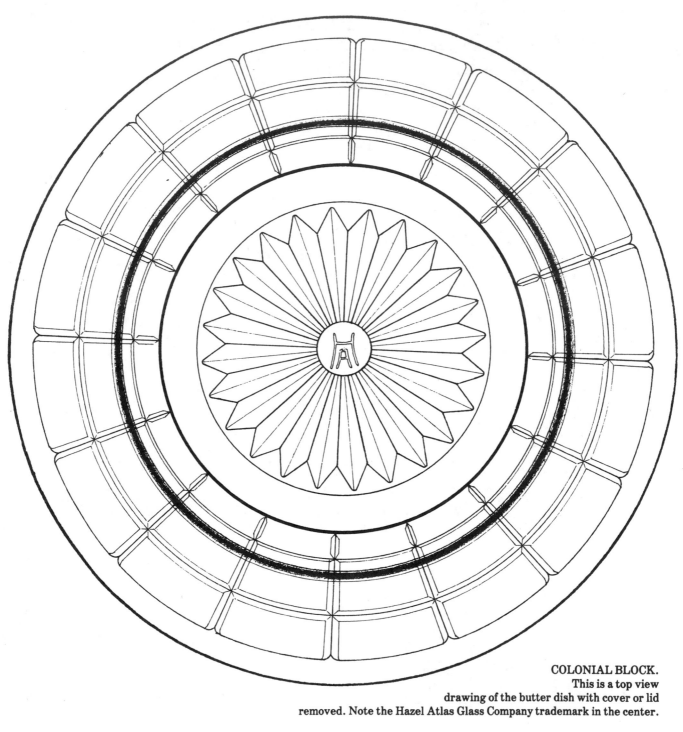

COLONIAL BLOCK.
This is a top view
drawing of the butter dish with cover or lid
removed. Note the Hazel Atlas Glass Company trademark in the center.

Colors found to date:

• Green                    • Pink                    • White*

*1950's production only.  Value ranges from $4.00 to $7.50.

42

# COLONIAL BLOCK

**Reproductions or reissues**

None known to date.

**General pattern notes**

This is a relatively minor pattern of Depression glass. Its inclusion is because of its similarity to the Block Optic pattern and the butter dish frequently being mistaken for Block Optic.

| ITEM & DESCRIPTION | DOLLAR VALUE RANGES BY COLOR |
| --- | --- |
| | Green or Pink |
| Bowl, 4" | 8-10 |
| Bowl, 7" | 18-20 |
| Butter dish | 55-60 |
| Candy jar (covered) | 45-50 |
| Creamer | 12-15 |
| Sugar and cover | 24-28 |

# COLONIAL FLUTED

c. 1930

Federal Glass Company
Columbus, Ohio

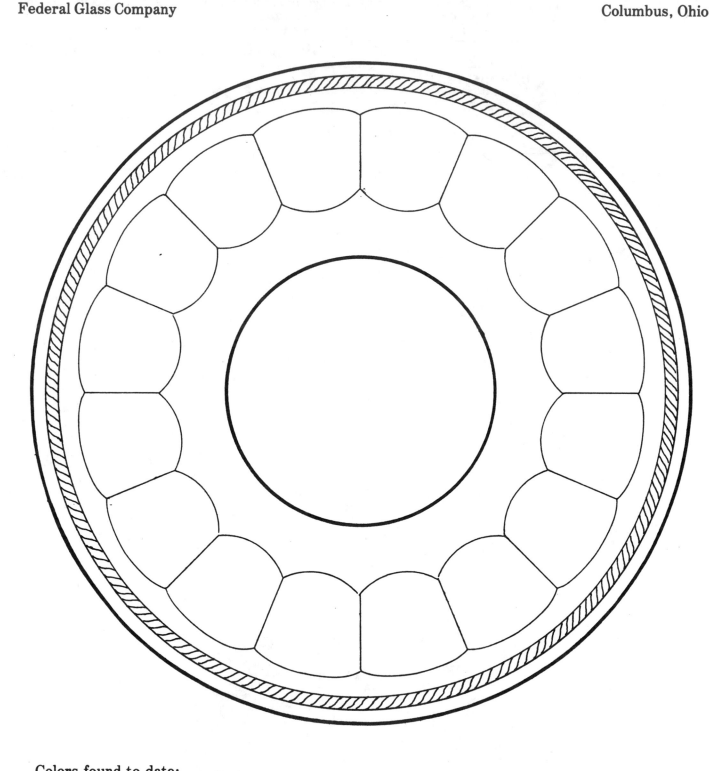

**Colors found to date:**

- Crystal
- Green
- Pink

# COLONIAL FLUTED

**Reproductions or reissues**

None known to date.

**General pattern notes**

Federal has made it easy to spot its products by frequently, but not always, using its trademark. It is easily recognizable when it appears—an "F" within a shield.

The pattern is also known as "Rope" because of the rope-like border design.

There has been no dinner plate size found so far that can be truly labeled Colonial Fluted. There is another Federal Glass Company design that is quite similar, but it lacks the rope border design described above. Whether it is Colonial Fluted has to be a matter of the collector's personal opinion until further evidence is found.

A particularly attractive variation in the pattern is "The Bridgette Set." These are six pieces that can be found with hearts, diamonds, clubs, and spades fired on the plates in red and black enamel.

| ITEM & DESCRIPTION | DOLLAR VALUE RANGES BY COLOR |
|---|---|
|  | Green |
| Bowl, 4" | 8-10 |
| Bowl, 6" | 10-12 |
| Bowl, 6-1/2" | 20-24 |
| Bowl, 7-1/2" | 20-24 |
| Creamer | 8-10 |
| Cup | 6-8 |
| Plate, 6" | 6-8 |
| Plate, 8" | 6-8 |
| Saucer | 3-5 |
| Sherbet | 6-8 |
| Sugar and cover | 20-24 |

# COLUMBIA

1938 - early 1940 s

Federal Glass Company

Columbus, Ohio

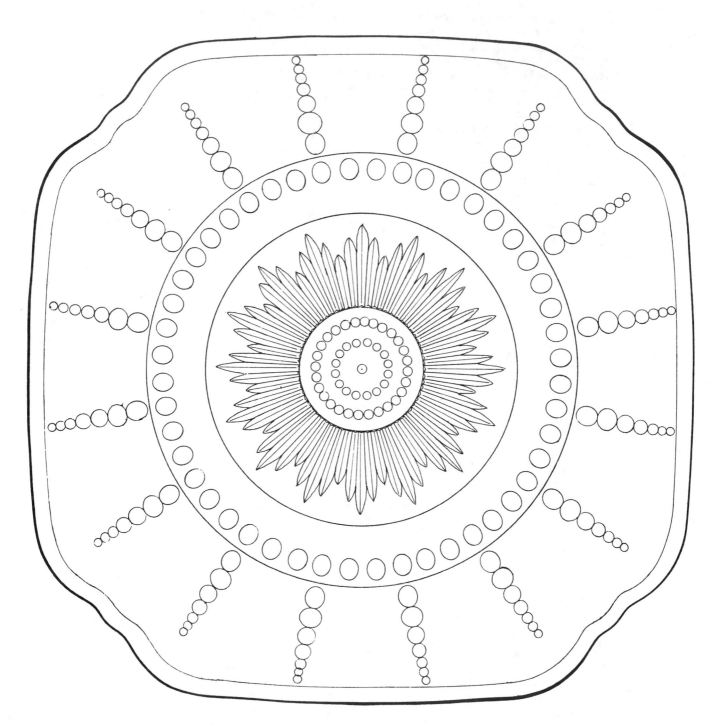

**Colors found to date:**

- Crystal
- Green
- Pink

# COLUMBIA

**Reproductions or reissues**

None known to date.

**General pattern notes**

First issued in pink in 1938, it quickly was changed to crystal. There are, therefore, few pink pieces to be found. Indeed, only four pieces were made in pink (see listing). Others in this pattern may be found with gold rims and various color decorations on butter-dish covers.

| ITEM & DESCRIPTION | DOLLAR VALUE RANGES BY COLOR | |
| --- | --- | --- |
| | Crystal | Pink |
| Bowl, 5" | 18-20 | — |
| Bowl, 8" | 24-26 | — |
| Bowl, 8-1/2" | 22-24 | — |
| Bowl, 10-1/2" (ruffled edge) | 24-26 | — |
| Butter dish and cover | 24-26 | — |
| Cup | 6-8 | 10-12 |
| Plate, 6" | 4-6 | 8-10 |
| Plate, 9-1/2" | 8-10 | 20-24 |
| Plate, 11-3/4" | 10-24 | — |
| Saucer | 1-2 | 8-10 |
| Snack plate | 20-24 | — |
| Tumbler, 4 oz. | 20-24 | — |
| Tumbler, 9 oz. | 28-30 | — |

# CORONATION

## 1936 - 1940

Hocking Glass Company                    (now Anchor-Hocking Glass Corporation)

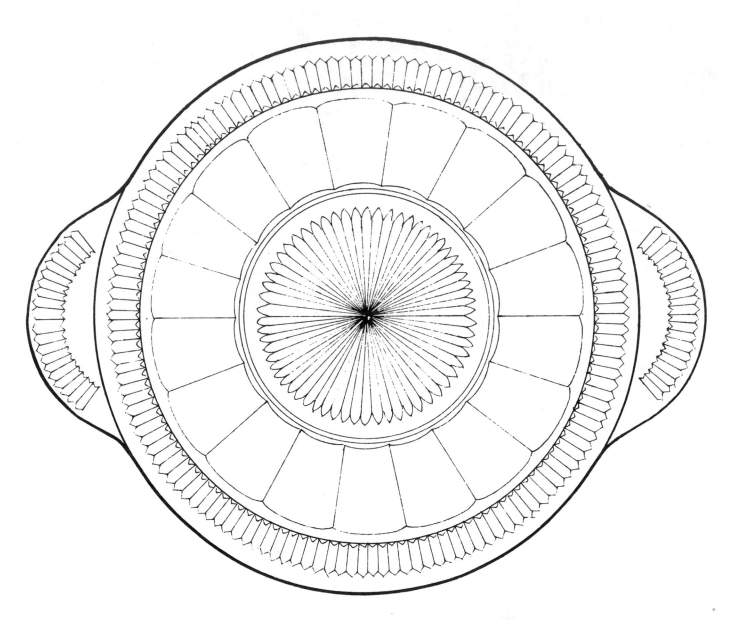

CORONATION. Drawing shows top view of a 4½" berry bowl with closed handles (no holes in the handles). The same bowl can be found with open handles. The bowl pattern design remains the same but the pattern design in the handles differs slightly from that of the closed handle bowls.

### Colors found to date:

- Crystal          - Pink          - Ruby Red

# CORONATION

**Reproductions or reissues**

   None known to date.

**General pattern notes**

   Be very careful not to confuse the tumblers in this pattern with "Lace Edge" pattern tumblers. This frequently causes much inconvenience in buying or trading among dealers and collectors alike. The ray designs in the Coronation pattern tumblers ascend much farther up the side than do those on the Lace Edge tumblers.

   The handles on ruby-red bowls are almost always open.

| ITEM & DESCRIPTION | DOLLAR VALUE RANGES BY COLOR | |
| --- | --- | --- |
| | Pink | Red |
| Bowl, 4-1/4" | 6-8 | 8-10 |
| Bowl, 6-1/2" | 8-10 | 14-16 |
| Bowl, 8", handle | 14-16 | 20-24 |
| Cup | 6-8 | 8-10 |
| Pitcher | 450-500 | — |
| Plate, 6" | 4-6 | — |
| Plate, 8-1/2" | 12-14 | 14-16 |
| Saucer | 4-6 | — |
| Sherbet | 6-8 | — |
| Tumbler, 5" (footed) | 30-35 | — |

# CUBIST
**1929 - 1933**

Jeannette Glass Company

Jeannette, Pennsylvania

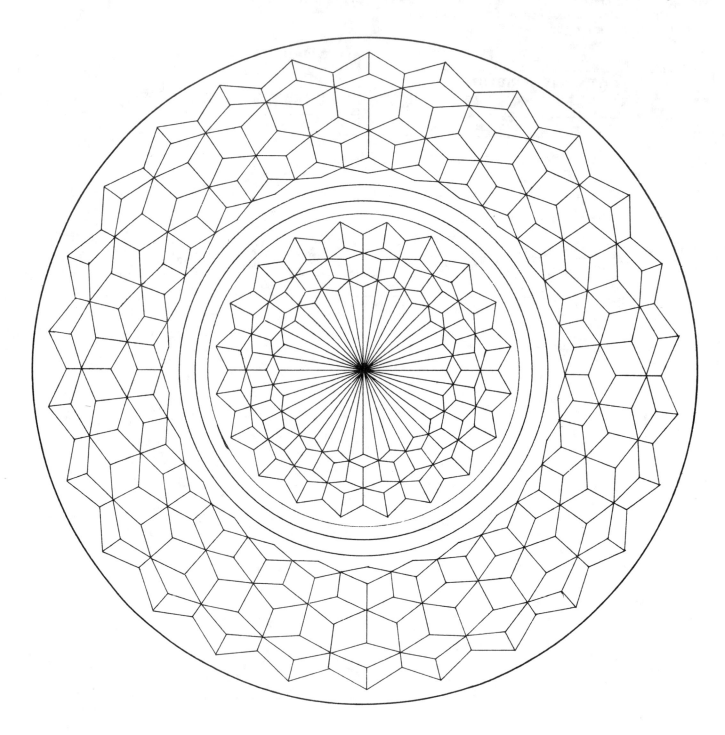

Colors found to date:

- Crystal
- Green
- Pink

# CUBIST

**Reproductions or reissues**
None found to date.

**General pattern notes**
The first thing the collector should be aware of is the extreme similarity between this pattern and the very fine **crystal** pattern "American" by Fostoria. Should you have crystal items in your collection that do not match any of those listed below, then it is probably Fostoria. The Depression-glass pattern of Cubist is nearly the same, but the quality is far below that of Fostoria crystal.

The green color wasn't in production long so it isn't easy to find. Crystal was the last color to be added to the line.

The candy and sugar lids in Cubist are the same and are interchangeable.

| ITEM & DESCRIPTION | DOLLAR VALUE RANGES BY COLOR | |
| --- | --- | --- |
| | Green | Pink |
| Bowl, 4-1/2" | 8-10 | 6-8 |
| Bowl, 4-1/2" deep | 10-12 | — |
| Bowl, 6-1/2 | 18-20 | 16-18 |
| Butter dish and cover | 85-95 | 75-85 |
| Candy jar and cover, 6-1/2" | 45-55 | 40-45 |
| Coaster | 10-12 | 8-10 |
| Creamer, 2" | — | 6-8 |
| Creamer, 3" | 10-12 | 8-10 |
| Cup | 10-12 | 8-10 |
| Pitcher, 8-3/4" | 225-250 | 200-225 |
| Plate, 6" | 10-12 | 8-10 |
| Plate, 8" | 14-16 | 12-14 |
| Powder jar and cover (three-legged) | 30-35 | 30-35 |
| Salt and pepper (pair) | 40-45 | 40-45 |
| Saucer | 4-5 | 4-5 |
| Sherbet (footed) | 10-12 | 8-10 |
| Sugar, 2" | — | 6-8 |
| Sugar, 3" | 10-12 | 8-10 |
| Sugar or candy (covered) | 20-22 | 20-22 |
| Tray for 3" creamer and sugar, 7-1/2" (crystal) | — | — |
| Tumbler, 4" | 65-75 | 60-65 |

# DAISY

Indiana Glass Company

Dunkirk, Indiana

Colors found to date:

- Amber
- Crystal
- Dark Green

# DAISY

**Reproductions or reissues**

None known to date.

**General pattern notes**

This pattern was called "No. 620" by the company. Daisy is the name given it by collectors.

The green color, and some white pieces even, are there to be found, but collectors should know that these colors are of the 1960s and 1970s vintage and therefore not Depression glass. The crystal color is the most popular color; amber was made during the 1940s.

| ITEM & DESCRIPTION | DOLLAR VALUE RANGES BY COLOR | |
| --- | --- | --- |
| | Amber | Crystal or Green |
| Bowl, 4-1/2" | 8-10 | 4-5 |
| Bowl, 4-1/2 (cream soup) | 10-12 | 5-6 |
| Bowl, 6" | 24-26 | 8-10 |
| Bowl, 7-3/8" | 14-16 | 6-8 |
| Bowl, 9-3/8" | 24-26 | 8-10 |
| Bowl, 10" (oval) | 16-18 | 8-10 |
| Creamer (footed) | 8-10 | 4-6 |
| Cup | 4-6 | 3-5 |
| Plate, 6" | 4-5 | 2-3 |
| Plate, 7-3/8" | 5-6 | 3-4 |
| Plate, 8-3/8" | 5-6 | 3-4 |
| Plate, 9-3/8" | 8-10 | 4-6 |
| Plate, 10-3/8" (grill) | 6-8 | 4-6 |
| Plate, 11-1/2" (sandwich) | 14-16 | 6-8 |
| Platter, 10-3/4" | 12-14 | 6-8 |
| Relish dish (three sections) | 24-26 | 10-12 |
| Saucer | 2-4 | 1-4 |
| Sherbet (footed) | 6-8 | 4-5 |
| Sugar (footed) | 8-10 | 4-6 |
| Tumbler, 9 oz. (footed) | 16-18 | 8-10 |
| Tumbler, 12 oz. (footed) | 35-40 | 14-16 |

# DIAMOND QUILTED

## c. 1930

Imperial Glass Company

Bellaire, Ohio

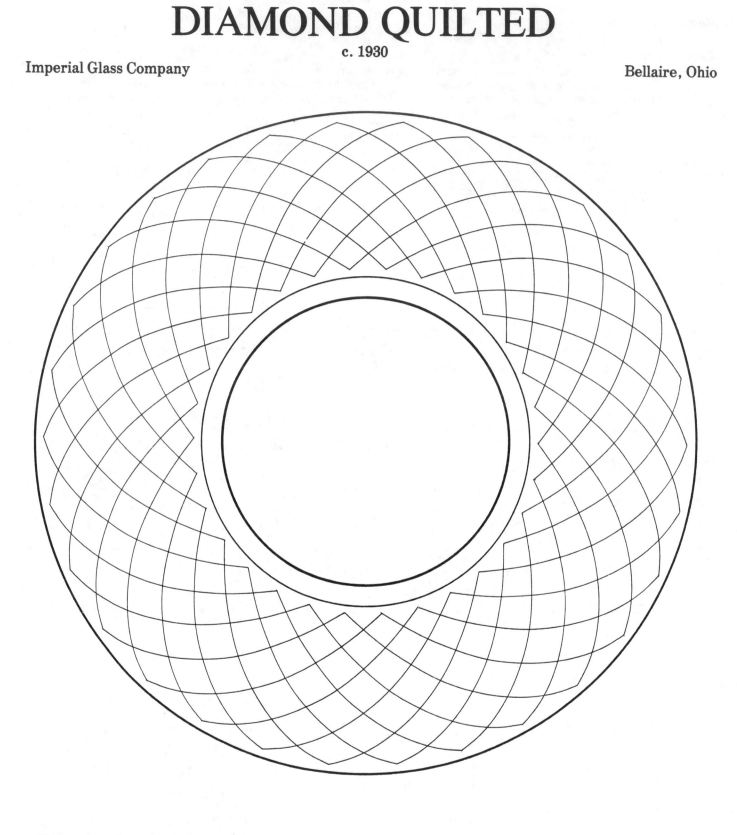

**Colors found to date:**

- Black
- Blue
- Crystal
- Green
- Pink

# DIAMOND QUILTED

## Reproductions or reissues
None known to exist.

## General pattern notes
Sometimes known as "Flat Diamond," this pattern was only proven to be a product of Imperial in the recent past.
The large punch bowl with stand and the champagne bucket are on the top of the scarce list for this pattern.
Sometimes the pattern appears on the bottom of the black pieces, so turn it over when investigating black tableware.

| ITEM & DESCRIPTION | DOLLAR VALUE RANGES BY COLOR | |
|---|---|---|
| | **Black or Blue** | **Green or Pink** |
| Bowl, 4-3/4" (cream soup) | 18-20 | 12-14 |
| Bowl, 5" | 16-18 | 8-10 |
| Bowl, 5-1/2" (one-handled) | 16-18 | 8-10 |
| Bowl, 7" | 18-20 | 12-14 |
| Bowl (rolled edge), 10-1/2" | 45-50 | 28-30 |
| Bowl, 6-1/4" (covered, footed) | 30-35 | 30-35 |
| Bowl, 7-1/4" (footed) | 30-35 | 30-35 |
| Bowl, 7-1/2 (footed) | 30-35 | 30-35 |
| Cake salver (10" in diameter) | — | 45-50 |
| Candlesticks (pair) | 45-50 | 30-35 |
| Candy jar and cover | — | 85-95 |
| Compote and cover, 11-1/2" | — | 100-125 |
| Creamer | 16-18 | 10-12 |
| Cup | 16-18 | 10-12 |
| Goblet, 1 oz. | — | 10-12 |
| Goblet, 2 oz. | — | 10-12 |
| Goblet, 3 oz. | — | 8-10 |
| Goblet, 9 oz. (champagne) | — | 10-12 |
| Ice bucket | 75-85 | 60-65 |
| Mayonnaise set (ladle, plate, three-footed dish) | 50-55 | 35-40 |
| Pitcher, large, 64 oz. | — | 55-60 |
| Plate, 6" | 6-8 | 4-6 |
| Plate, 7" | 10-12 | 6-8 |
| Plate, 8" | 12-14 | 10-12 |
| Punch bowl with stand | — | 400-450 |
| Plate, 14" | — | 18-20 |
| Sandwich server (center-handled) | 45-50 | 30-35 |
| Saucer | 4-5 | 4-5 |
| Sherbet | 12-14 | 10-12 |
| Sugar | 16-18 | 10-12 |
| Tumbler, 9 oz. | — | 8-10 |
| Tumbler, 12 oz. | — | 16-18 |
| Tumbler, 6 oz. (footed) | — | 8-10 |
| Tumbler, 9 oz. (footed) | — | 12-14 |
| Tumbler, 12 oz. (footed) | — | 16-18 |
| Vase (dolphin handles) | 75-85 | 45-50 |
| Whiskey jigger, 1-1/2 oz. | — | 12-15 |

# DIANA
## 1933 - 1941

Federal Glass Company

Columbus, Ohio

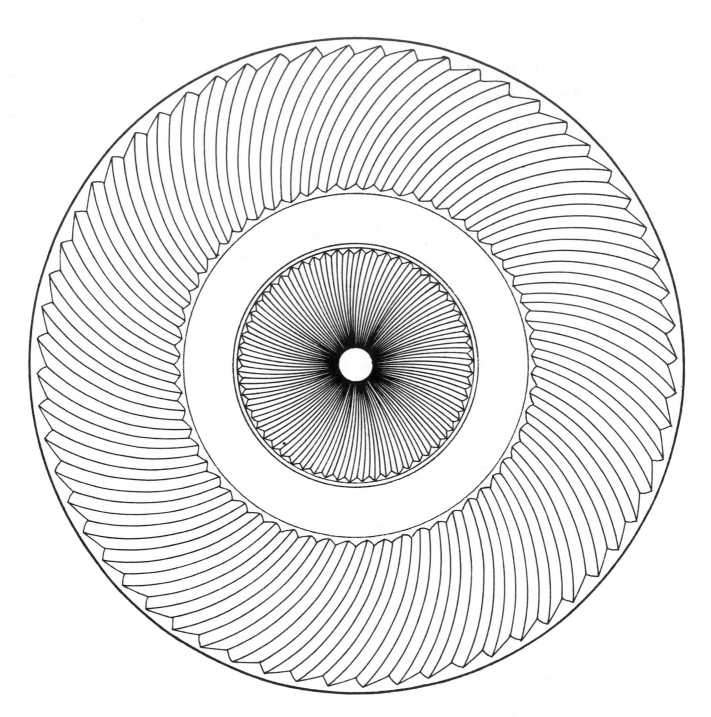

**Colors found to date:**

- Amber
- Crystal
- Pink

# DIANA

## Reproductions or reissues
The 11" console bowl has been reproduced.

## General pattern notes
First issued in 1933, it was apparently removed from the line sometime later and placed back into production in 1937.
Few odd pieces were made other than the coaster, ashtray, and the small demitasse set.
Some frosted pieces have begun appearing.

| ITEM & DESCRIPTION | DOLLAR VALUE RANGES BY COLOR |
| --- | --- |
| | Amber, Crystal, or Pink |
| Ashtray, 3-1/2" | 2-5 |
| Bowl, 5" | 5-10 |
| Bowl, 5-1/2", cream soup | 5-20 |
| Bowl, 9" | 8-20 |
| Bowl, 11" (console) | 8-35 |
| Bowl, 12" (scalloped edge) | 12-35 |
| Candy jar (covered) | 14-45 |
| Coaster, 3-1/2" | 2-10 |
| Creamer | 4-10 |
| Cup | 4-10 |
| Cup, 2 oz. demitasse and 4-1/2" saucer (set) | 8-45 |
| Plate, 6" | 2-8 |
| Plate, 9-1/2" | 4-18 |
| Plate, 11-3/4" | 8-20 |
| Platter, 12" (oval) | 8-30 |
| Salt and pepper (pair) | 24-85 |
| Saucer | 2-6 |
| Sherbet | 3-10 |
| Sugar (no cover) | 2-10 |
| Tumbler, 4-1/8" | 8-40 |
| Junior set (6 cups, saucers, plates with upright round rack) | 75-295 |

# DOGWOOD
### 1930 - 1934

Macbeth-Evans Glass Company

Charleroi, Pennsylvania

Colors to be found:

- Cremax
- Crystal*
- Green
- Monax
- Pink
- Yellow*

*Not commonly found. Odd pieces only.

# DOGWOOD

**Reproductions or reissues**

None known to date.

**General pattern notes**

This pattern is sometimes called "Apple Blossom" or "Wild Rose" by a few collectors, but the pattern is definitely a dogwood motif. The design is usually molded in the typical fashion, but there have been some rare occurrences of a "silk-screen" acid etched look, usually on pitchers.

Some of the sectioned "grill" style plates have been found with the center design absent. The big 12-inch oval platter is the most difficult to find, as well as the most valuable.

A few of the pieces were quite fragile, in that the glass was a bit too thin. So the molds were redesigned to produce a thicker walled piece. Both are still found.

| ITEM & DESCRIPTION | DOLLAR VALUE RANGES BY COLOR | | |
| --- | --- | --- | --- |
| | Green | Monax or Cremax | Pink |
| Bowl, 5-1/2" | 35-40 | 8-10 | 30-35 |
| Bowl, 8-1/2" | 110-125 | 30-35 | 60-65 |
| Bowl, 10-1/4" | 245-275 | 85-95 | 450-500 |
| Cake plate, 11" | — | — | 1,000-1,200 |
| Cake plate, 13" | 100-125 | 85-95 | 125-145 |
| Creamer, 2-1/2" (thin walled) | 45-50 | — | 30-35 |
| Creamer, 3-1/4" (thick walled) | — | — | 20-24 |
| Cup | 40-45 | 24-26 | 28-30 |
| Pitcher, 8", 80 oz. | 550-575 | — | 200-250 |
| Pitcher, 8", 80 oz. (American Sweetheart shape) | — | — | 600-650 |
| Plate, 6" | 10-12 | 20-24 | 8-10 |
| Plate, 8" | 12-14 | — | 10-12 |
| Plate, 9-1/4" | — | — | 35-40 |
| Plate, 10-1/2" (grill, either design) | 24-26 | — | 24-26 |
| Plate, 12" (salver) | — | 15-18 | 35-40 |
| Platter, 12" (oval) | — | — | 650-695 |
| Saucer | 8-10 | 14-16 | 8-10 |
| Sherbet (footed) | 100-125 | — | 35-40 |
| Sugar, 2-1/2" (thin walled) | 45-50 | — | 30-35 |
| Sugar, 3-1/4" (thick walled) | — | — | 20-24 |
| Tumbler, 3-1/2" | — | — | 250-300 |
| Tumbler, 4" | 95-100 | — | 45-50 |
| Tumbler, 4-3/4" | 110-125 | — | 50-60 |
| Tumbler, 5" | 125-135 | — | 85-95 |
| Tumbler (etched band) | — | — | 22-24 |
| Tidbit (8" and 12" plates with metal spindle) | 40-50 | — | 45-60 |

# DORIC and PANSY — DORIC

**1937 - 1938**  **1935 - 1938**

Jeannette Glass Company  Jeannette, Pennsylvania

This drawing represents **two** different patterns. The upper half is the "Doric and Pansy",
the lower half is "Doric".

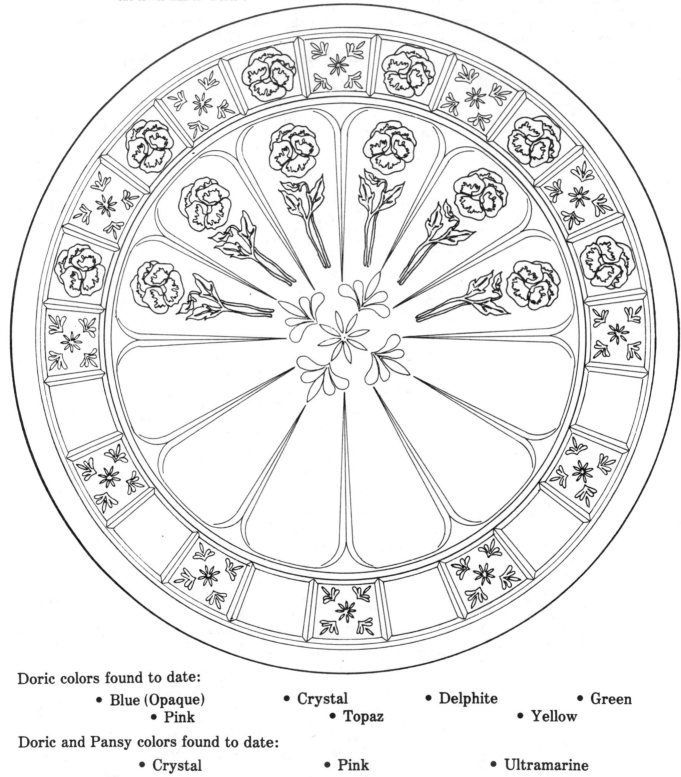

Doric colors found to date:

- Blue (Opaque)  • Crystal  • Delphite  • Green
  - Pink  • Topaz  • Yellow

Doric and Pansy colors found to date:

- Crystal  • Pink  • Ultramarine

# DORIC

## Reproductions or reissues
None known to date.

## General pattern notes
Pink, green, and delphite are the three colors most commonly found. The others occur rarely and are very difficult to place values upon. If you find any iridescent pieces, they are likely of recent vintage.

Occasionally, you may find a flower etched on every other panel of the 10-inch sandwich tray.

| ITEM & DESCRIPTION | DOLLAR VALUE RANGES BY COLOR | | |
|---|---|---|---|
| | Delphite | Green | Pink |
| Bowl, 4-1/2" | 45-50 | 8-10 | 8-10 |
| Bowl, 5" (cream soup) | — | 400-450 | — |
| Bowl, 5-1/2" | — | 85-95 | 85-95 |
| Bowl, 8-1/4" | 125-135 | 30-35 | 28-30 |
| Bowl, 9" (two-handled) | — | 20-24 | 20-24 |
| Bowl, 9" (oval) | — | 38-40 | 30-35 |
| Butter dish (covered) | — | 95-100 | 85-95 |
| Cake plate, 10" (three legs) | — | 28-30 | 26-28 |
| Candy dish and cover, 8" | — | 40-45 | 35-40 |
| Candy dish (three sections) | 18-20 | 12-15 | 12-15 |
| Coaster, 3" | — | 16-18 | 16-18 |
| Creamer, 4" | — | 18-20 | 18-20 |
| Cup | — | 8-10 | 8-10 |
| Pitcher, 6" | 1,100-1,300 | 45-50 | 38-40 |
| Pitcher, 7-1/2" (footed) (in yellow, it's $600) | — | 1,000-1,200 | 650-700 |
| Plate, 6" | — | 6-8 | 6-8 |
| Plate, 7" | — | 24-26 | 18-20 |
| Plate, 9" | — | 20-24 | 18-20 |
| Plate, 9" (grill) | — | 28-30 | 24-26 |
| Platter, 12" (oval) | — | 30-35 | 28-30 |
| Relish tray (square), 4" x 4" | — | 12-14 | 10-12 |
| Relish tray, 4" x 8" | — | 18-20 | 16-18 |
| Salt and pepper | — | 40-45 | 40-45 |
| Saucer | — | 4-5 | 4-5 |
| Sherbet (footed) | 10-12 | 18-18 | 14-16 |
| Sugar and cover | — | 45-50 | 30-35 |
| Tray, 10" (handled, sandwich plate) | — | 20-24 | 18-20 |
| Tray, 8" x 8" | — | 35-40 | 28-30 |
| Tumbler, 4-1/2", 9 oz. | — | 95-100 | 65-75 |
| Tumbler, 4", 11 oz. | — | 75-85 | 60-65 |
| Tumbler, 5", 12 oz. | — | 125-135 | 75-85 |

# DORIC and PANSY
## (Pattern illustration on Page 60)

### Reproductions or reissues
None known to date.

### General pattern notes
Doric and Pansy remains a difficult pattern to collect. All colors are scarce. The ultramarine is usually what you encounter when you find it. As with the pink color in the Jeannette products, so does this ultramarine vary widely in hue, so don't let it fool you if the colors don't exactly match.

A highly sought set in Doric and Pansy is the child's set called "Pretty Polly Party Dishes." It is a 14-piece set.

| ITEM & DESCRIPTION | DOLLAR VALUERANGES BY COLOR | |
| --- | --- | --- |
| | Crystal or Pink | Ultramarine |
| Bowl, 4-1/2" | 12-14 | 18-20 |
| Bowl, 8" | 30-35 | 85-95 |
| Bowl, 9" (handled) | 20-24 | 35-40 |
| Butter dish and cover | — | 450-500 |
| Cup | 12-15 | 16-18 |
| Creamer | 65-75 | 100-125 |
| Plate, 6" | 8-10 | 14-16 |
| Plate, 7" | — | 45-50 |
| Plate, 9" | 14-16 | 35-40 |
| Salt and pepper (pair) | — | 350-400 |
| Saucer | 4-6 | 8-10 |
| Sugar (no cover) | 50-60 | 150-175 |
| Tray, 10" (handled) | — | 30-35 |
| Tumbler, 4-1/2" | — | 110-125 |
| "PRETTY POLLY PARTY DISHES" | | |
| Creamer | 35-40 | 60-65 |
| Cup | 30-35 | 45-50 |
| Plate | 8-10 | 18-20 |
| Saucer | 4-5 | 10-12 |
| Sugar | 35-40 | 60-65 |
| Entire 14-piece set | 240-280 | 320-450 |

# ENGLISH HOBNAIL

### 1925 - late 1970 s

Westmoreland Glass Company                    Graperville, Pennsylvania

ENGLISH HOBNAIL.  Make a close
comparison to the MISS AMERICA pattern and make
careful note of the differences.  They are explained in the text accompanying each listing.

## Colors found to date:

- Amber
- Blue
- Cobalt
- Crystal
- Green
- Pink
- Red
- Turquoise

# ENGLISH HOBNAIL

## Reproductions or reissues

None known to date.

## General pattern notes

This could well be one of the most confusing of the patterns to collect, but it is also one of the more beautiful, so perhaps worth the study necessary to master the complexities.

The pattern was first released in amber and crystal in 1925. In 1929-30, Westmoreland introduced a variation of crystal by adding black stems to some footed pieces. It also added blue, green, and pink to the line around 1926 or so. It goes on and on. A whole book could be devoted to the identification and dating of all the different colors and pieces added over the years.

Westmoreland consistently produced the crystal tableware from the beginning and right into the 1970s, when even more colors were added. In the 1960s, it added another hue of amber, but only the well-versed collector and dealer can distinguish between the two. The company closed in 1983.

To alleviate any confusion, the collector might well collect it without regard to vintage, but only for its beauty.

Values are only a bit higher than the highest range of average. The value list presented here is not classified as to color and is only a sampling of different items available. They very likely approach several hundred in number when different colors and variations due to design change are taken into account.

Be sure to note the similarity of English Hobnail to Miss America. The principal difference is in the lengths of the rays in the center design. The rays in Miss America are uniform in length. Those in English Hobnail are in varying lengths.

Values for turquoise and cobalt colors are 100-200 percent higher than those listed below.

| ITEMS & DESCRIPTION | DOLLAR VALUE RANGES BY COLOR |
| --- | --- |
| | All Colors |
| Ashtray (various shapes) | 5-20 |
| Bowls, 6" (various styles) | 8-20 |
| Bowls, 8" (various styles) | 12-30 |
| Candlesticks, 3-1/2" (pair) | 20-40 |
| Candlesticks, 8-1/2" (pair) | 30-60 |
| Celery dish, 9" | 20-35 |
| Demitasse cup and saucer | 25-65 |
| Goblets (several issues) | 8-35 |
| Lamp, 9-1/4" | 40-140 |
| Pitcher, 23 oz. | 50-145 |
| Pitcher, 60 oz. | 85-300 |
| Plate, 6-1/2" (pie) | 6-10 |
| Plate, 10" | 15-45 |
| Salt and pepper (pair) | 30-150 |
| Saucer | 3-8 |
| Tumbler, 4" | 10-20 |
| Tumbler, 5" | 12-24 |
| Tumbler, 7 oz. (footed) | 10-20 |
| Tumbler, 9 oz. (footed) | 12-24 |
| Tumbler, 12 oz. (footed) | 12-30 |
| (This tumbler has also been found with both round (common) and square-footed bases) | |
| Whiskey jiggers, 1-1/2 oz. and 3 oz. | 12-20 |

# FLORAGOLD

1950 s

Jeanette Glass Company                                    Jeanette, Pennsylvania

Colors found to date:

- Iridescent        • Crystal        • Blue        • Pink

# FLORAGOLD

**Reproduction or reissues**

None found to date.

**General pattern notes**

Floragold is also known by collectors as Louisa. The most commonly found color is the iridescent amber. This is the first color made, with the others being of a later vintage. The rarest piece is the vase. It looks like a large footed tumbler with a ruffled or scalloped upper edge.

| ITEM & DESCRIPTION | DOLLAR VALUE RANGES BY COLOR |
| --- | --- |
| | Iridescent |
| Bowl, 4-1/2", squared | 6-8 |
| Bowl, 5-1/2", round | 50-60 |
| Bowl, 5-1/2", ruffled | 6-8 |
| Bowl, 8-1/2", squared | 18-20 |
| Bowl, 9-1/2", ruffled | 8-10 |
| Bowl, 9-1/2", straight sided | 45-50 |
| Bowl, 12", ruffled | 10-12 |
| Butter dish, covered, 1/4 lb., oblong | 45-50 |
| Butter dish, covered, round | 50-60 |
| Candlestick (pair), two-branched | 70-75 |
| Candy, 6-3/4", covered | 50-60 |
| Candy, 5-1/4", four-footed | 6-8 |
| Candy, single handled | 10-12 |
| Creamer | 10-12 |
| Cup | 5-6 |
| Pitcher, 64 oz. | 35-45 |
| Plate, 5-3/4" | 8-10 |
| Plate, 8-1/2" | 40-45 |
| Plate, 11-1/4" | 24-26 |
| Plate, 13-1/2" | 24-26 |
| Plate or tray, 13-1/2", partitioned | 60-65 |
| Salt and pepper, plastic tops | 60-65 |
| Saucer, 5-1/4" | 6-8 |
| Sherbet, footed | 12-14 |
| Sugar, covered | 20-24 |
| Tumbler, 10 oz. | 20-24 |
| Tumbler, 11 oz. | 24-28 |
| Tumbler, 15 oz. | 100-125 |

# FLORAL
### 1930 - 1937

Jeannette Glass Company

Jeannette, Pennsylvania

Colors found to date:

- Crystal
- Jadite
- Delphite
- Pink
- Green

# FLORAL

## Reproductions or reissues

There exists a very good reproduction of each of the salt and pepper shakers.

## General pattern notes

This pattern is also sometimes called "poinsettia." The colors listed on Page 67 are more typical ones, although some very isolated pieces have been found in yellow, amber, and red. These should be considered rare, unless, or until, more are found. They may be isolated instances of experimental production, therefore limited in quantity.

The delphite items were made for a short time, being introduced during 1937, the last year of Floral production.

A couple of unusual sets have surfaced: a set of three covered bowls in a tray, called a "dresser set," and another, a six-inch utility tray with a ribbed surface.

Look for the design motif beneath the covers on opaque colored items with covers.

Candy lids and sugar lids are identical.

| ITEM & DESCRIPTION | DOLLAR VALUE RANGES BY COLOR | | |
| --- | --- | --- | --- |
| | Delphite | Green | Pink |
| Bowl, 4" | 45-50 | 24-28 | 20-24 |
| Bowl, 5-1/2" (cream soup) | — | 650-700 | 650-700 |
| Bowl, 7-1/2" | 70-75 | 30-35 | 30-35 |
| Bowl, 8" (covered) | 75-85 | 60-65 | 60-65 |
| Bowl, 9" (oval) | — | 28-30 | 24-26 |
| Butter dish and cover | — | 95-100 | 100-125 |
| Canister set (four-piece in Jadeite only: 85-95) | — | — | — |
| Candlesticks, 4" (pair) | — | 85-95 | 75-85 |
| Candy jar and cover | — | 45-50 | 45-50 |
| Creamer | 65-75 | 18-20 | 16-18 |
| Coaster | — | 12-14 | 14-16 |
| Compote, 9" | — | 950-1000 | 800-850 |
| Cup | — | 12-14 | 14-16 |
| Dresser set | — | 1,400-1,600 | — |
| Ice tub, 3-1/2" (oval) | — | 850-900 | 800-850 |
| Lamp | — | 250-275 | 225-250 |
| Pitcher, 5-1/2" | — | 550-575 | — |
| Pitcher, 8" (footed, cone shaped) | — | 45-50 | 50-55 |
| Pitcher, 10-1/4" | — | 350-375 | 275-300 |
| Plate, 6" | — | 6-8 | 6-8 |
| Plate, 8" | — | 14-16 | 12-14 |
| Plate, 9" | 125-150 | 20-22 | 18-20 |
| Plate, 9" (grill) | — | 250-275 | — |
| Platter, 10-3/4" (oval) | 150-175 | 20-24 | 18-20 |
| Refrigerator dish and cover, 5" x 5" (Jadeite: 30-35) | — | 65-75 | 60-65 |
| Relish dish (oval, two sections) | — | 20-22 | 18-20 |
| Salt and pepper, 4" (footed) | — | 55-60 | 50-55 |
| Salt and pepper, 6" | — | — | 50-55 |
| Saucer | — | 8-10 | 8-10 |
| Sherbet | 95-100 | 22-24 | 18-20 |
| Sugar | 50-60 | 10-12 | 10-12 |
| Sugar or candy and cover | 75-85 | 35-40 | 35-40 |

| ITEM & DESCRIPTION | DOLLAR VALUE RANGES BY COLOR | | |
|---|---|---|---|
| | Delphite | Green | Pink |
| Tray, 6" | — | 30-35 | 28-30 |
| Tumbler, 4-1/2" | — | 175-185 | |
| Tumbler, 3-1/2 (footed) | — | 195-225 | |
| Tumbler, 4" (footed) | — | 24-26 | 24-26 |
| Tumbler, 4-3/4 (footed) | 175-195 | 28-30 | 28-30 |
| Tumbler, 5-1/4" (footed) | — | 55-60 | 50-55 |
| Vase (rose bowl, three-legged) | — | 650-750 | |
| Vase (flared, three-legged) | — | 600-650 | |
| Vase, 6-7/8" | — | 650-700 | |
| Flower frogs (for vases) | — | 500-600 | |

Note: The sugar or candy cover has not yet been seen in delphite. It may or may not have been produced. If found, this value would be much, much higher.

# FLORAL and DIAMOND BAND

c. 1930

U. S. Glass Company                                    *Pittsburgh, Pennsylvania

Colors found to date:

- Black          • Blue          • Green
  • Iridescent              • Pink

*The company had numerous locations for factories.  Pittsburgh was one of the only two locations still operating in 1938.

# FLORAL AND DIAMOND BAND

**Reproductions or reissues**

None known to date.

**General pattern notes**

The collector should take particular note that there have been no cups and saucers found in this pattern and no evidence any were ever produced.

Green is the predominant color encountered, with pink following. The other colors should be considered fairly scarce and worth considerably more.

This is another pattern that has a heavy, quality feel unusual to typical Depression glass items.

There is no significant difference between the pink and green items, although you might have to pay 10-20 percent more for the green.

| ITEM & DESCRIPTION | DOLLAR VALUE RANGES BY COLOR |
|---|---|
| | Green or Pink |
| Bowl, 4-1/2" | 8-10 |
| Bowl, 5-3/4" (handled) | 12-14 |
| Bowl, 8" | 16-18 |
| Butter dish and cover | 125-145 |
| Compote, 5-1/2" | 18-20 |
| Creamer (small) | 8-10 |
| Creamer, 4-3/4" | 16-18 |
| Pitcher, 8" | 110-125 |
| Plate, 8" | 35-40 |
| Sherbet | 8-10 |
| Sugar (small) | 8-10 |
| Sugar and cover, 5-1/4" | 65-75 |
| Tumbler, 4" | 24-28 |
| Tumbler, 5" | 50-60 |

# FLORENTINE NUMBER ONE

### 1932 - 1935

Hazel Atlas Glass Company

Clarksburg, West Virginia and Zanesville, Ohio

FLORENTINE NO. 1. This drawing actually represents the pattern for FLORENTINE NO. 2 also. Please refer to the text of both pattern listings for an explanation of the difference.

Colors found to date:

- Cobalt
- Crystal
- Green
- Pink
- Yellow

# FLORENTINE NUMBER ONE

**Reproductions or reissues**

These are reproductions of the footed salt and pepper shakers to be found.

**General pattern notes**

This pattern is also frequently called "Old Florentine" and sometimes "Poppy No. 1."

Many of the items in the line are flanged and flat-rimmed with five distinct sides.

There is another quite similar pattern, "Florentine No. 2," on the following pages. The two patterns are easily confused by collectors, although the pattern on the Florentine No. 1 is very obviously rendered smaller than that of the No. 2 on the larger pieces. The chief difference to look for is that No. 1 has five-sided pieces and all the pieces in No. 2 are round and have no serrations. This is true regarding all pieces, except the pitchers on which the patterns appear to be the same.

Blue (cobalt) pieces are the most rare.

| ITEM & DESCRIPTION | DOLLAR VALUE RANGES BY COLOR | | |
|---|---|---|---|
| | Crystal or Green | Pink | Yellow |
| Ashtray, 5-1/2" | 15-22 | 28-30 | 28-30 |
| Bowl, 5" (blue: 18-23) | 10-12 | 14-16 | 14-16 |
| Bowl, 6" | 12-20 | 28-30 | 28-30 |
| Bowl, 8-1/2" | 12-20 | 32-35 | 32-35 |
| Bowl, 9-1/2" (oval, with cover) | 40-55 | 65-75 | 65-75 |
| Butter dish and cover | 100-135 | 165-170 | 165-175 |
| Coaster or ashtray, 3-3/4" | 15-20 | 26-28 | 20-22 |
| Creamer | 6-10 | 18-20 | 16-18 |
| Creamer (ruffled edge) (blue: 60-75) | 30-50 | 35-40 | — |
| Cup | 6-10 | 10-12 | 10-12 |
| Pitcher, 6-1/2" (footed) (blue: 505-580) | 30-40 | 45-50 | 45-50 |
| Pitcher, 7-1/2" | 60-85 | 125-150 | 175-200 |
| Plate, 6" | 5-8 | 10-12 | 10-12 |
| Plate, 8-1/2" | 8-12 | 12-15 | 12-15 |
| Plate, 10" | 12-18 | 24-26 | 24-26 |
| Plate, 10" (grill) | 8-12 | 12-15 | 12-15 |
| Platter, 11-1/2" (oval) | 15-24 | 26-28 | 26-28 |
| Salt and pepper (footed) | 30-45 | 50-55 | 50-55 |
| Saucer | 1-4 | 4-5 | 4-5 |
| Sherbet (footed) | 8-12 | 12-14 | 12-14 |
| Sugar and cover | 20-30 | 32-35 | 32-35 |
| Sugar (ruffled edge) | 30-40 | 30-35 | — |
| Tumbler, 3-1/4" (footed) (blue: 60-70) | 12-18 | — | — |
| Tumbler, 3-3/4" (footed) | 12-18 | 24-26 | 24-26 |
| Tumbler, 4-3/4" (footed) | 15-22 | 26-28 | 26-28 |
| Tumbler, 5-1/4" (footed) | 20-30 | 30-32 | 30-32 |
| Tumbler, 5-1/4" | — | 100-125 | — |

# FLORENTINE NUMBER TWO

Manufactured from 1934-1937 by the Hazel Atlas Glass Company in Clarksburg, West Virginia, and Zanesville, Ohio.

## Colors found to date

Amber (yellow), blue, blue (cobalt), crystal, green, and pink.

## Reproductions or reissues

None known to date.

## General pattern notes

Please refer to Florentine No. 1 for pattern illustration and discussion of principal differences between these two patterns.
Footed pieces in Florentine No. 2 have round bases.
The two patterns mix together nicely, but many purist collectors wouldn't think of combining them.
Amber (yellow) and blue are the rare colors.

| ITEM & DESCRIPTION | DOLLAR VALUE RANGES BY COLOR | | |
|---|---|---|---|
| | Crystal or Green | Pink | Yellow |
| Ashtray, 3-3/4" | 14-20 | — | 26-30 |
| Ashtray, 5-1/2" | 14-20 | — | 35-38 |
| Bowl, 4-1/2" | 10-16 | 16-18 | 18-20 |
| Bowl, 4-3/4" (cream soup) | 12-18 | 18-20 | 20-24 |
| Bowl, 5" (blue: 35-45) | 14-22 | 24-26 | — |
| Bowl, 5-1/2" | 20-30 | — | 40-42 |
| Bowl, 6" | 24-32 | — | 38-40 |
| Bowl, 8" | 20-30 | 30-32 | 38-40 |
| Bowl, 9" (oval, with cover) | 45-60 | — | 75-85 |
| Bowl, 9" | 25-30 | — | — |
| Butter dish and cover | 100-125 | — | 185-195 |
| Candlesticks, 2-3/4" (pair) | 45-60 | — | 70-80 |
| Candy dish and cover | 100-125 | 145-155 | 165-175 |
| Coaster, 3-1/4" | 8-12 | 16-18 | 20-22 |
| Compote, 3-1/2" (ruffled edge) (blue: 66-76) | 30-45 | 12-15 | — |
| Creamer | 6-10 | — | 12-14 |
| Cup | 8-10 | — | 10-12 |
| Custard | 40-60 | — | 85-95 |
| Gravy boat | — | — | 60-70 |
| Pitcher, 6-1/4" (footed, cone shaped) (blue: 480-540) | — | — | 175-195 |
| Pitcher, 7-1/2" (footed, cone shaped) | 30-40 | — | 35-40 |
| Pitcher, 8" | 100-125 | 225-250 | 400-450 |
| Plate, 6" | 3-6 | — | 6-8 |
| Plate, 6-1/4", with indent | 14-20 | — | 30-35 |
| Plate, 8-1/2" | 6-10 | 8-10 | 8-10 |
| Plate, 10" | 10-16 | — | 18-20 |
| Plate, 10-1/4" (grill) | 8-14 | — | 16-18 |
| Platter, 11" (oval) | — | — | 50-60 |
| Relish dish, 10" (three sections) | 14-20 | 30-35 | 30-35 |
| Salt and pepper (pair) | 40-50 | — | 55-60 |
| Saucer | 2-6 | — | 4-6 |
| Sherbet (footed) | 10-12 | — | 12-14 |

| ITEM & DESCRIPTION | DOLLAR VALUE RANGES BY COLOR | | |
|---|---|---|---|
| | Crystal or Green | Pink | Yellow |
| Sugar and cover | 20-26 | — | 28-30 |
| Tray (for shakers, creamer and sugar, round) | — | — | 85-95 |
| Tumbler, 3-1/2" (two styles) | 8-12 | 12-14 | 20-22 |
| Tumbler, 4" (blue: 60-75) | 10-15 | 18-20 | 18-20 |
| Tumbler, 5" (flat, blown) | 20-26 | — | — |
| Tumbler, 3-1/4" (footed) | 12-15 | 18-20 | 20-22 |
| Tumbler, 4" (footed) | 10-15 | — | 18-20 |
| Tumbler, 4-1/2" (footed) | 20-30 | — | 38-40 |
| Tumbler, 5" (flat, ice tea) | 30-40 | — | 55-60 |
| Vase, 6" | 30-40 | — | 65-70 |

# FLOWER GARDEN WITH BUTTERFLIES
## 1920's-1930's

U.S. Glass Company

Pittsburgh, Pennsylvania

Colors found to date:

- Amber
- Black
- Blue
- Crystal
- Green
- Pink
- Blue-green

# FLOWER GARDEN WITH BUTTERFLIES

**Reproduction or reissues**

None found to date.

**General pattern notes**

This pattern is also known as Butterflies and Roses. You may have to look hard to find the butterflies, for they are relatively obscure. There is almost always at least one to be found somewhere in the design, although it has been reported that it can be found without it altogether on rare occasions. This pattern is difficult to locate and the prices are rising at a phenomenal rate. The rarest piece is the heart-shaped covered candy.

| ITEM & DESCRIPTION | DOLLAR VALUE RANGES BY COLOR |
|---|---|
| | All Colors |
| Ashtray, has cigarette and match holders | 150-195 |
| Bowl, rolled edge, two types | 200-250 |
| Bowl, 10", footed | 250-300 |
| Candlestick (pair), 4" | 85-100 |
| Candlestick (pair), 8" | 95-200 |
| Candy, 8", covered | 80-195 |
| Candy, heart shape, covered | 1000-1250 |
| Cheese and cracker plate, 10", and compote, 4" | 300-400 |
| Cigarette box, 3-1/2" x 2-1/2" | 150-200 |
| Cologne, 7-1/2", footed, stoppered | 200-300 |
| Creamer | 75-100 |
| Cup | 65-75 |
| Mayonnaise, three-piece set | 75-145 |
| Plate, 7" | 14-30 |
| Plate, 8", two designs | 20-30 |
| Powder jar | 75-125 |
| Powder jar, footed | 75-200 |
| Sandwich plate, center handled | 50-125 |
| Saucer | 20-30 |
| Sugar, no cover | 75-100 |
| Tray, 10" x 5-1/2", oval | 50-60 |
| Tray, 11-3/4" x 7-3/4", rectangular | 50-80 |
| Vase, 6" | 75-150 |
| Vase, 7" | 140-175 |
| Vase, 10" | 150-195 |

# FOREST GREEN
## 1950s-1967

Anchor-Hocking Glass Corporation

Lancaster, Ohio
Long Island City, New York

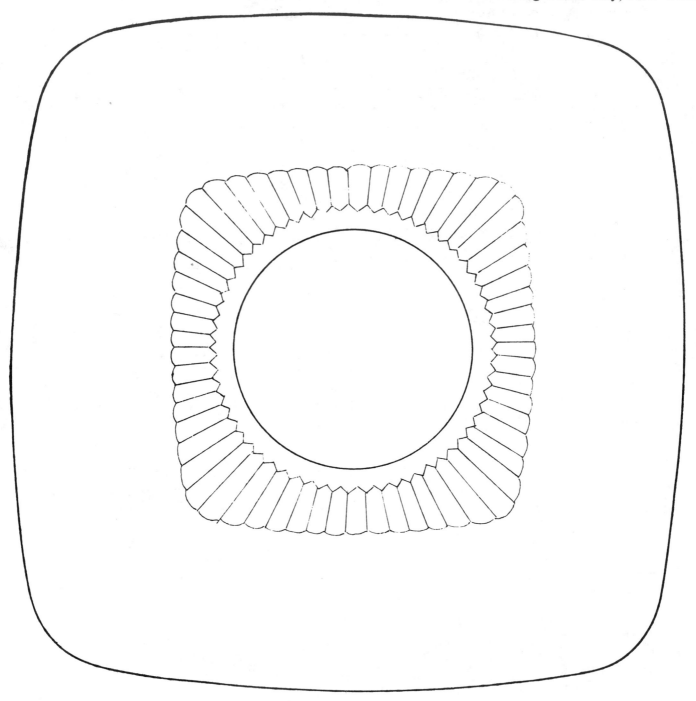

Colors found to date:

• Green only

# FOREST GREEN

## Reproductions or reissues

None known to date.

## General pattern notes

Although, strictly speaking, this is not Depression era glassware, Forest Green is very popular among collectors; hence, included here. It was introduced soon after Hocking Glass acquired the Anchor Cap and Closure Company and became Anchor-Hocking. The pattern utilized many of Hocking's molds for the older Royal Ruby pattern. As a general rule, most of the pieces in both patterns are the same. The squared pieces were introduced much later than the others (see accompanying illustration). These squared pieces each have the ribbed design in the center. The other items have little or no ornamentation and are quite plain. The vibrant green and red (Royal Ruby) are the outstanding characteristics of both patterns.

| ITEM & DESCRIPTION | DOLLAR VALUE RANGES |
|---|---|
| Ashtray | 6-8 |
| Bowl, 4-3/4" | 8-10 |
| Bowl, 6" | 10-12 |
| Bowl, 7-1/4" | 16-18 |
| Creamer | 6-8 |
| Cup | 4-5 |
| Mixing bowls, three-piece set | 30-35 |
| Mixing bowls, no lip or spout | 10-12 |
| Pitcher, 22 oz. | 24-28 |
| Pitcher, three quart | 30-35 |
| Plate, 6-1/2" | 6-8 |
| Plate, 8-1/2" | 8-10 |
| Plate, 10" | 26-28 |
| Platter, rectangular | 22-24 |
| Punch bowl with stand | 75-85 |
| Punch cup | 4-5 |
| Saucer | 1-2 |
| Sugar | 6-8 |
| Tumblers, two sizes | 6-8 |
| Vase, Ball-type | 5-6 |
| Vase, 6-1/2" | 8-10 |
| Vase, 9" | 18-20 |

# FORTUNE

### 1936 - 1938

Hocking Glass Company

(now Anchor-Hocking Glass Corporation)

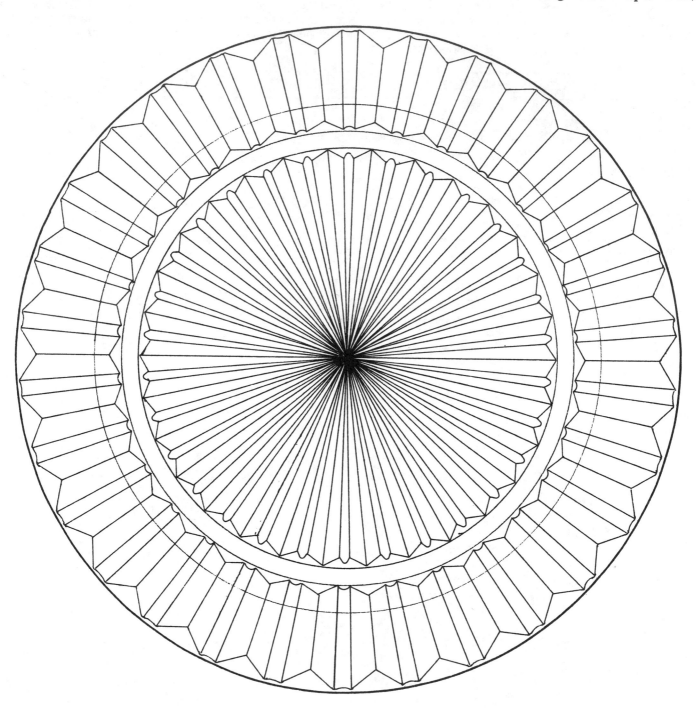

Colors found to date:

- Crystal
- Pink

# FORTUNE

**Reproductions or reissues**

None known to date.

**General pattern notes**

Made as a cereal promotion pattern, there are not many pieces out there and available to collectors. The eight-inch luncheon plates are the most difficult to locate.

| ITEM & DESCRIPTION | DOLLAR VALUE RANGES BY COLOR |
|---|---|
| | Crystal or Pink |
| Bowl, 4" | 6-8 |
| Bowl, 4-1/2" | 8-10 |
| Bowl, 4-1/2" (handled) | 8-10 |
| Bowl, 5-1/4" (rolled edge) | 16-18 |
| Bowl, 7-3/4" | 18-20 |
| Candy dish and cover | 30-35 |
| Cup | 8-10 |
| Plate, 6" | 6-8 |
| Plate, 8" | 22-24 |
| Saucer | 2-4 |
| Tumbler, 3-1/2" | 12-15 |
| Tumbler, 4" | 16-18 |

# FRUITS

1930 s

Manufacture attributed to several companies.

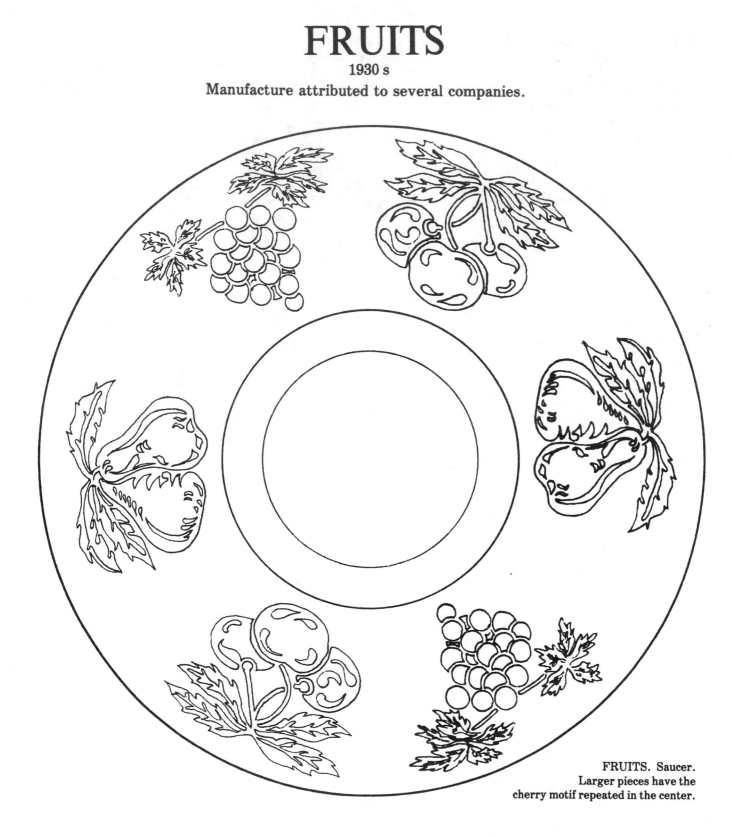

FRUITS. Saucer.
Larger pieces have the
cherry motif repeated in the center.

Colors found to date:

- Crystal
- Green
- Pink

# FRUITS

**Reproductions or reissues**

None known to date.

**General pattern notes**

This is a pattern that is simple and attractive. Few pieces are known to exist—11 types in all.

Because Fruits was made by several different companies, the fruits may vary somewhat and in the case of some of the tumblers, there are some very desirable ones that bear the cherry motif only. There have been reports of some iridescent pieces surfacing.

| ITEMS & DESCRIPTION | DOLLAR VALUE RANGES BY COLOR |
|---|---|
| | Green or Pink |
| Bowl, 5" | 24-35 |
| Bowl, 8" | 45-75 |
| Cup | 10-12 |
| Pitcher, 7" | 90-100 |
| Plate, 8" | 10-12 |
| Saucer | 3-4 |
| Sherbet | 10-12 |
| Tumbler, 3-1/2" | 50-60 |
| Tumbler, 4" (cherries or pears only) | 25-28 |
| Tumbler, 4" | 18-20 |
| Tumbler, 5" | 125-150 |

# GEORGIAN
### 1931 - 1936

Federal Glass Company

Columbus, Ohio

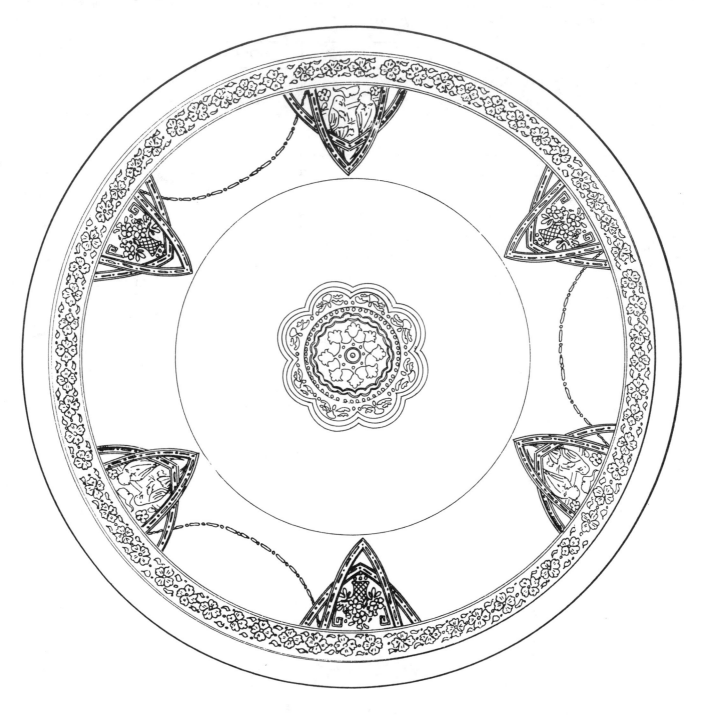

Colors found to date:

- Crystal
- Green

# GEORGIAN

**Reproductions or reissues**

None known to date.

**General pattern notes**

This pattern is also popularly known as "Love Birds."

An unusual piece to be found is the wooden lazy Susan, 18-1/4 inches. It has seven sections in which the six-inch hot-plate dishes are to be placed. A complete set of the lazy Susan and plates would be valued in the mid- to high-hundreds of dollars.

Dinner plates are found with the full design and also with the edge design (no center design and no love birds or baskets). The tumblers exhibit baskets only in the design and the lids of the sugars have only the edge design present. The other covered pieces have complete lid designs.

| ITEM & DESCRIPTION | DOLLAR VALUE RANGES BY COLOR |
|---|---|
| | Green |
| Bowl, 4-1/2" | 8-10 |
| Bowl, 5-3/4" | 28-30 |
| Bowl, 6-1/2" | 75-80 |
| Bowl, 7-1/2" | 65-75 |
| Bowl, 9" (oval) | 65-75 |
| Butter dish and cover | 85-95 |
| Creamer, 3" (footed) | 14-16 |
| Creamer, 4" (footed) | 18-20 |
| Cup | 12-14 |
| Hot plate, 5" (center design) | 85-95 |
| Plate, 6" | 8-10 |
| Plate, 8" | 12-14 |
| Plate, 9-1/4" | 34-36 |
| Plate, 9-1/4" (center design) | 26-28 |
| Platter, 11-1/2" (closed handles) | 75-85 |
| Saucer | 4-6 |
| Sherbet | 16-18 |
| Sugar and cover, 3" (footed) | 40-45 |
| Sugar and cover, 4" (footed) | 100-125 |
| Tumbler, 4" | 50-60 |
| Tumbler, 5-1/4" | 85-95 |

# HARP

1950 s

Jeanette Glass Company

Jeanette, Pennsylvania

Colors found to date:

- Crystal
- Light Blue
- Crystal with Gold rims

# HARP

**Reproductions and reissues**

None known to date.

**General pattern notes**

Little is known about the number of pieces to be found in this pattern. It appears to be limited as you may note from the listing below. It looks as if it might have been made only as a party or hostess set due to the small number and type of pieces that have so far been found.

| ITEM & DESCRIPTION | DOLLAR VALUE RANGES BY COLOR |
|---|---|
| | Crystal |
| Ashtray-coaster combination, 4-3/4" x 3-1/4" | 8-10 |
| Coaster | 6-8 |
| Cup | 20-24 |
| Saucer | 2-4 |
| Cake stand, 9" high | 20-24 |
| Plate, 7-1/4" | 16-18 |
| Tray, rectangular | 32-34 |
| Vase, 6" | 28-30 |

# HERITAGE
## c. 1940 s

Federal Glass Company

Columbus, Ohio

**Colors found to date:**

- Blue
- Crystal
- Green
- Pink

# HERITAGE

**Reproductions or reissues**

None are known to date.

**General pattern notes**

The crystal is the most common, with the other colors only occasionally being found. From time to time, the collector may find some with gold edge trim.

Values for pink are about three times, and blue and green are roughly five times the values for crystal listed below.

| ITEM & DESCRIPTION | DOLLAR VALUE RANGES BY COLOR |
|---|---|
| | Crystal |
| Bowl, 5" | 4-5 |
| Bowl, 8-1/2" | 18-20 |
| Bowl, 10-1/2" | 12-15 |
| Cup | 6-8 |
| Creamer (footed) | 24-28 |
| Plate, 8" | 8-10 |
| Plate, 9-1/4" | 12-14 |
| Plate, 12" | 14-16 |
| Saucer | 2-3 |
| Sugar (footed) | 24-28 |

# HEX OPTIC or HONEYCOMB

### 1928 - 1932

Federal Glass Company

Columbus, Ohio

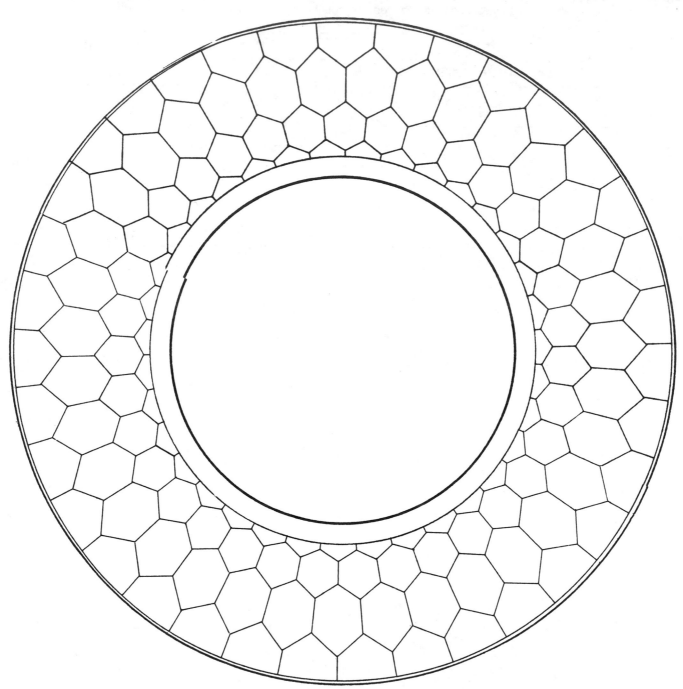

**Colors found to date:**

• Green        • Pink

# HEX OPTIC or HONEYCOMB

**Reproductions or reissues**

None known to date.

**General pattern notes**

This pattern is known by both names above about equally, although "Hex Optic" is also used as a generic term to describe a type of pattern made by many different companies. "Honeycomb" is therefore preferable.

Tumblers and pitchers appeared in iridescent in the 1960s.

May have been made by other companies also.

| ITEM & DESCRIPTION | DOLLAR VALUE RANGES BY COLOR |
|---|---|
| | Green or Pink |
| Bowl, 4-1/4" | 6-8 |
| Bowl, 7-1/2" | 8-10 |
| Bowl, 7-1/4" | 10-12 |
| Bowl, 8-1/4" | 16-18 |
| Bowl, 9" | 18-20 |
| Bowl, 10" | 24-28 |
| Butter dish and cover (rectangular) | 35-40 |
| Creamer (two styles) | 85-95 |
| Cup (two styles) | 8-10 |
| Ice bucket | 8-10 |
| Ice bucket (metal handle) | 30-40 |
| Pitcher, 5" (sunflower in bottom) | 24-26 |
| Pitcher, 9" (footed) | 45-50 |
| Plate, 6" | 4-6 |
| Plate, 8" | 6-8 |
| Platter, 11" | 18-20 |
| Refrigerator dish, 4" | 15-18 |
| Refrigerator stack set (three pieces) | 85-95 |
| Salt and pepper (pair) | 30-40 |
| Saucer | 2-3 |
| Sugar (two styles) | 8-10 |
| Sherbet, 5 oz. (footed) | 8-10 |
| Tumbler, 3-3/4" | 6-8 |
| Tumbler, 5-3/4" (footed) | 10-12 |
| Tumbler, 7" (footed) | 12-15 |
| Whiskey jigger, 2" | 8-10 |

# HOBNAIL

## 1934 - 1936

Hocking Glass Company

(now Anchor-Hocking Glass Corporation)

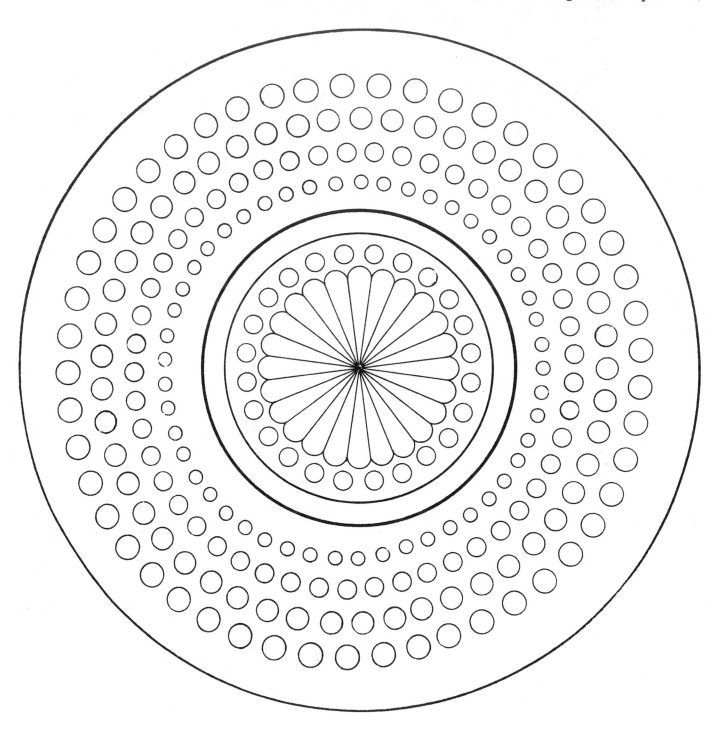

Colors found to date:

• Crystal

• Pink

# HOBNAIL

**Reproductions or reissues**

None known.

**General pattern notes**

Collectors should be aware that the "Moonstone" pattern, found on later pages in this book, is virtually the same pattern design with a few additions of ornament and some different type pieces.

Crystal is the most common of the two colors, with the pink being relatively scarce.

There are some crystal pieces with a very attractive red edge trim. This apparently is present only on luncheon sets.

Hobnail was made in some of the old molds, as far as is known, into the late 1960s. These are all in opaque white.

| | DOLLAR VALUE RANGES BY COLOR |
| --- | --- |
| **ITEM & DESCRIPTION** | **Crystal or Pink** |
| Bowl, 5-1/2" | 3-6 |
| Bowl, 7" | 4-8 |
| Cup | 2-6 |
| Creamer (footed) | 2-6 |
| Decanter and stopper | 20-35 |
| Goblet, 10 oz. | 6-10 |
| Goblet, 13 oz. | 6-10 |
| Goblet, 10 oz. | 15-24 |
| Pitcher, 67 oz. | 20-35 |
| Plate, 6" | 3-6 |
| Plate, 8-1/2" | 4-8 |
| Saucer | 1-3 |
| Sherbet | 2-5 |
| Sugar (footed) | 2-6 |
| Tumbler, 5 oz. | 2-6 |
| Tumbler, 9 oz. | 4-8 |
| Tumbler, 10 oz. | 4-8 |
| Tumbler, 15 oz. | 10-15 |
| Tumbler, 3 oz. (footed) | 4-8 |
| Tumbler, 5 oz. (footed) | 4-8 |
| Whiskey jigger, 1-1/2 oz. | 4-8 |

# HOLIDAY
## 1947 - 1949

Jeannette Glass Company

Jeannette, Pennsylvania

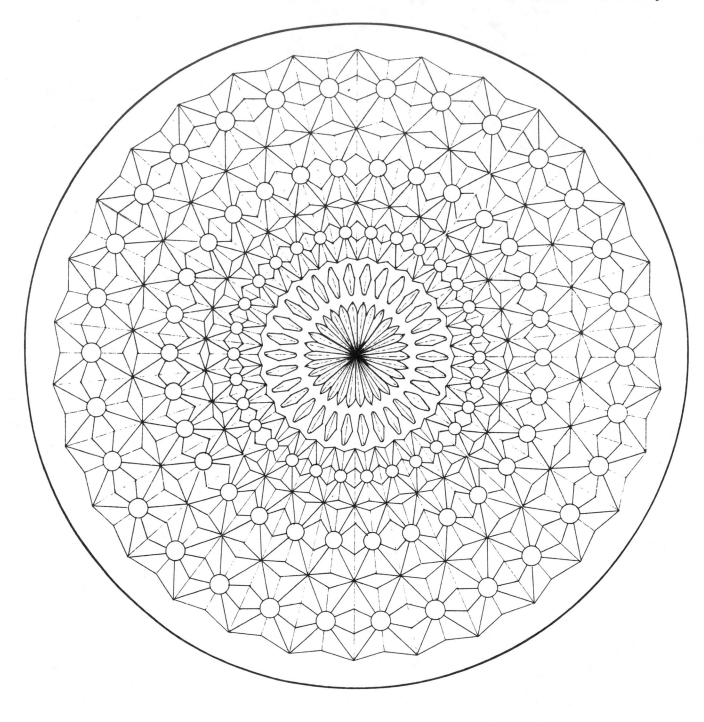

**Colors found to date:**

- Crystal
- Pink
- Shell Pink
- White (opaque)

# HOLIDAY

**Reproductions or reissues**
None known.

**General pattern notes**
A very intricate geometric design that flows nicely in spite of the straight lines and acute angles, this pattern is also known as "Buttons and Bows."

Pink is by far the most commonly found and collected color in the pattern. Some white and iridescent pieces were produced in the later days of manufacture and a shell pink piece was also offered. The latter, a console, and 16-oz. milk pitchers are considered very desirable by the collector, but the shell pink is an elusive catch.

There are two different types of cups to be found in Holiday.

| | DOLLAR VALUE RANGES BY COLOR |
|---|---|
| **ITEM & DESCRIPTION** | **Pink** |
| Bowl, 5-1/8" | 10-12 |
| Bowl, 7-3/4" | 45-50 |
| Bowl, 8-1/2" | 30-35 |
| Bowl, 9-1/2" (oval) | 24-26 |
| Bowl, 10-3/4" (console) | 95-110 |
| Butter dish and cover | 65-75 |
| Cake plate, 10-1/2" (three-legged) | 85-95 |
| Candlesticks, 3" (pair) | 85-95 |
| Creamer (footed) | 10-12 |
| Cup (two sizes) | 8-10 |
| Pitcher, 4-3/4" | 65-75 |
| Pitcher, 6-3/4" | 45-50 |
| Plate, 6" | 6-8 |
| Plate, 9" | 16-18 |
| Plate, 13-3/4" (salver) | 95-110 |
| Platter, 11-3/8" (oval) | 28-30 |
| Sandwich tray (10-1/2") | 20-24 |
| Saucer (two styles) | 4-6 |
| Sherbet | 8-10 |
| Sugar and cover | 40-45 |
| Tumbler, 4" | 18-20 |
| Tumbler, 4" (footed) | 35-40 |
| Tumbler, 6" (footed) | 125-145 |

# HOMESPUN

### 1938 - 1940

Jeannette Glass Company

Jeannette, Pennsylvania

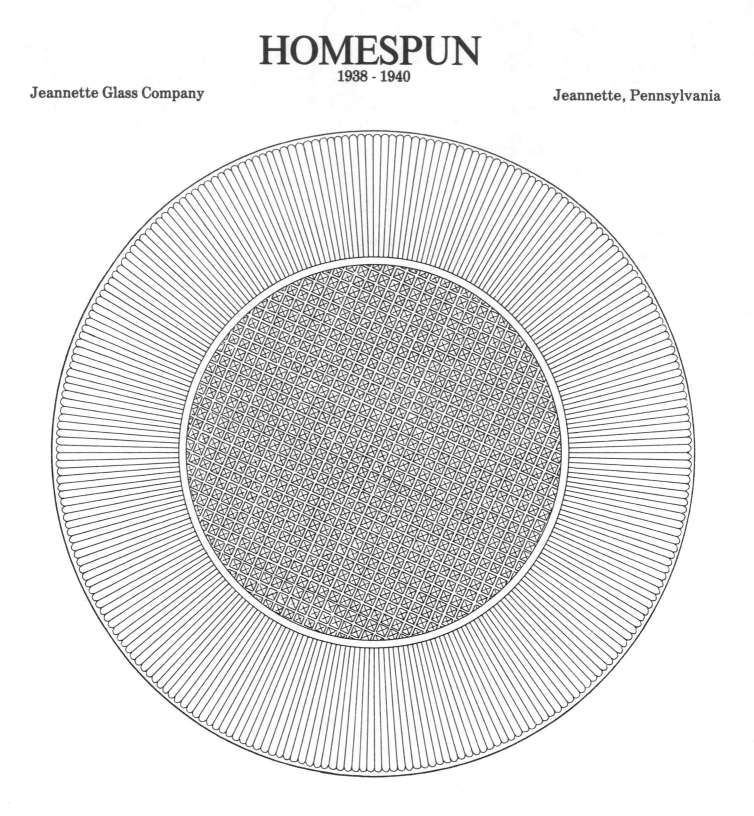

**Colors found to date:**

- Crystal
- Pink

Adam, pink footed pitcher, 8" high.

Swirl pieces in ultramarine. Back center: 8" diameter plate; back right: 5-1/2" diameter bowl; in the front, from left, are a cup and saucer, sugar bowl, and 6" diameter footed bowl.

Doric, green covered butter dish.

Patrician (Spoke), in amber. At left is a cup and saucer; back right: 9.4" diameter dinner plate; front: comport.

Iris and Herringbone, crystal. In back, from left, are a 7-1/2" diameter plate and a 9" diameter dinner plate. In front, from left: a 7" diameter soup bowl, 4-1/2" diameter fruit bowl, and cup and saucer.

Cubist, from left: pink 8-1/2" high pitcher and a green 8-1/2" high pitcher.

Lorain pieces in yellow. In the back is a 7-3/4" diameter plate. In the front, from left, are a cup and saucer, sherbet, and 4-3/4" high footed tumbler.

98

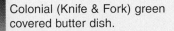
Colonial (Knife & Fork) green covered butter dish.

Moderntone, cobalt. In the back, from left, are a cup and saucer and 9" diameter dinner plate. In the front, from left, are a 6-1/2" diameter cereal bowl and a cream soup bowl.

New Century (Lydia Ray) green water pitcher, 8" high.

Florentine, in green. In the back is a 9-3/4" diameter plate and in front a cup and saucer.

Royal Lace, green, from left: footed creamer and footed covered sugar bowl.

Bubble, royal ruby, top left: 4-1/2" high 12-oz. tumbler; bottom left: 3-3/4" high 5-oz. tumbler; right: 9-1/4" high pitcher.

Parrot (Sylvan) amber cone sherbet.

Diana, crystal, at left: cup and saucer; right back: 9.4" diameter dinner plate; right front: cream soup bowl.

Moondrops, ice blue, back: crimped candle bowl; in front, from left: covered candy dish and double candlestick.

Cupid, pink, from left: 4.3" high sugar bowl and 4-1/2" high creamer.

Princess, green 8" diameter bowl.

Peacock and Wild Rose, amber, back: 10" diameter dinner plate; front: comport.

Bubble, light blue, in back: 11-3/4" long oval platter. In front, from left: 8-1/4" diameter bowl and cup and saucer.

Royal lace, cobalt, from left: cookie jar and 7.8" high pitcher.

Rose Cameo, green, 5" tall footed tumbler.

Sharon (Cabbage Rose), in back: pink cream soup bowl; in front, from left: pink rim soup bowl and green covered butter dish.

Jubilee, yellow, 7" diameter three-toed covered candy dish.

Dogwood, in back: crystal 12" long oval platter; front: green 9-3/4" diameter bowl.

English Hobnail, red candlesticks, 8" high.

Katy (Laced Edge), blue opalescent. In back: 9.4" diameter dinner plate; in front, from left: 7" diameter soup bowl; 4-1/2" diameter fruit bowl; and cup and saucer.

Clover Leaf, from left: green cup and saucer and yellow 6" high covered candy dish.

Anniversary, crystal, 9" high footed covered candy.

Holiday (Buttons and Bows), from left: pink 9" diameter plate, iridescent 3.8" high footed pitcher, and iridescent 4.8" high pitcher.

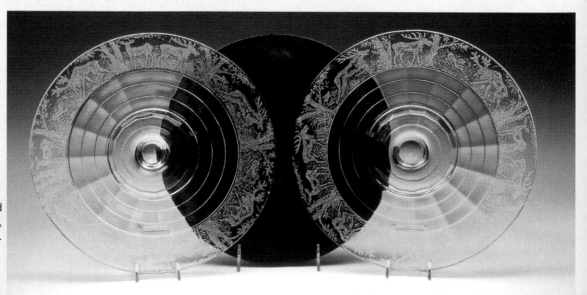

Black Forest, 11" diameter footed cake plates, from left: crystal, black, and green.

# HOMESPUN

## Reproductions or reissues

None known to date.

## General pattern notes

A very rare, large (96-ounce) pitcher exists in this pattern. A significant identifying characteristic of its design is that it does not have the characteristic waffle-like center design, only the fine ribbing design.

Another significant item is the tea set. The entire set of 14 pieces would bring around $350 or more, especially if it were to be found in the original packing box. The set is called "Homespun Tea Set." It is often referred to as a child's tea set. The crystal teapot is very rare. In fact, no one knows of one in a collection, but since the company advertised the sets as available in both colors, there is good reason to believe some lucky collector will eventually discover this treasure. Keep your eyeballs peeled and moving all the time on your hunts!

| ITEM & DESCRIPTION | DOLLAR VALUE RANGES BY COLOR |
| --- | --- |
| | Crystal or Pink |
| Bowl, 4-1/2" (closed handles) | 16-18 |
| Bowl, 5" | 28-30 |
| Bowl, 8-1/4" | 85-95 |
| Butter dish and cover | 8-10 |
| Coaster or ashtray | 12-14 |
| Creamer (footed) | 12-14 |
| Cup | 6-8 |
| Plate, 6" | 18-20 |
| Plate, 9-1/4" | 18-20 |
| Platter, 13" (closed handles) | 4-5 |
| Saucer | 18-20 |
| Sherbet | 12-14 |
| Sugar (footed) | 20-22 |
| Tumbler, 4" | 30-35 |
| Tumbler, 5-1/4" | 6-8 |
| Tumbler, 4" (footed) | 35-40 |
| Tumbler, 6-1/4" (footed) | 35-40 |
| Tumbler, 6-1/2" (footed) | |
| CHILD'S TEA SET | |
| Cup | 40-45 |
| Saucer | 20-24 |
| Dinner plate | 20-25 |
| Teapot | 65-75 |
| Teapot lid | 90-100 |

# HORSESHOE (No. 612)

## 1930 - 1933

Indiana Glass Company

Dunkirk, Indiana

**Colors to be found:**

• Crystal      • Green      • Pink      • Yellow

# HORSESHOE (No. 612)

## Reproductions or reissues
None are known to date.

## General pattern notes
To find crystal pieces in Horseshoe would be an exciting event indeed. They are so scarce that there is not sufficient trade data even to establish value, but it would be high compared to the rest of the pattern values.

Other rare pieces are the butter dish with cover, the pitcher, the covered candy dish with metal holder, and the grill plates.

There are some items without the center design. These are the candy dish and some of the plates.

| ITEM & DESCRIPTION | DOLLAR VALUE RANGES BY COLOR | |
| --- | --- | --- |
| | Green | Yellow |
| Bowl, 4-1/2" | 26-28 | 28-30 |
| Bowl, 6-1/2" | 28-30 | 32-35 |
| Bowl, 7-1/2" | 28-30 | 28-30 |
| Bowl, 8-1/2" | 35-38 | 35-38 |
| Bowl, 9-1/2" | 40-45 | 40-45 |
| Bowl, 10-1/2" (oval) | 35-38 | 35-38 |
| Butter dish and cover | 850-950 | — |
| Candy and cover with metal holder | 225-250 | — |
| Creamer (footed) | 18-20 | 22-24 |
| Cup | 8-10 | 12-14 |
| Pitcher, 8-1/2" | 350-400 | 400-450 |
| Plate, 6" | 8-10 | 8-10 |
| Plate, 8-3/8" | 12-15 | 12-15 |
| Plate, 9-3/8" | 12-15 | 12-15 |
| Plate, 10-3/8" | 20-24 | 18-20 |
| Plate, 10-3/8" (grill) | 85-95 | 95-110 |
| Plate, 11" | 24-26 | 24-26 |
| Platter, 10-3/4" (oval) | 28-30 | 35-40 |
| Relish (footed, three sections) | 24-26 | 30-35 |
| Saucer | 6-8 | 6-8 |
| Sherbet | 12-15 | 16-18 |
| Sugar (no cover) | 18-20 | 22-24 |
| Tumbler, 4-1/4" | 225-245 | — |
| Tumbler, 4-3/4" | 225-245 | — |
| Tumbler, 9 oz. (footed) | 28-30 | 30-35 |
| Tumbler, 12 oz. (footed) | 175-195 | 150-175 |

# IRIS
## 1928 - 1932

Jeannette Glass Company

Jeannette, Pennsylvania

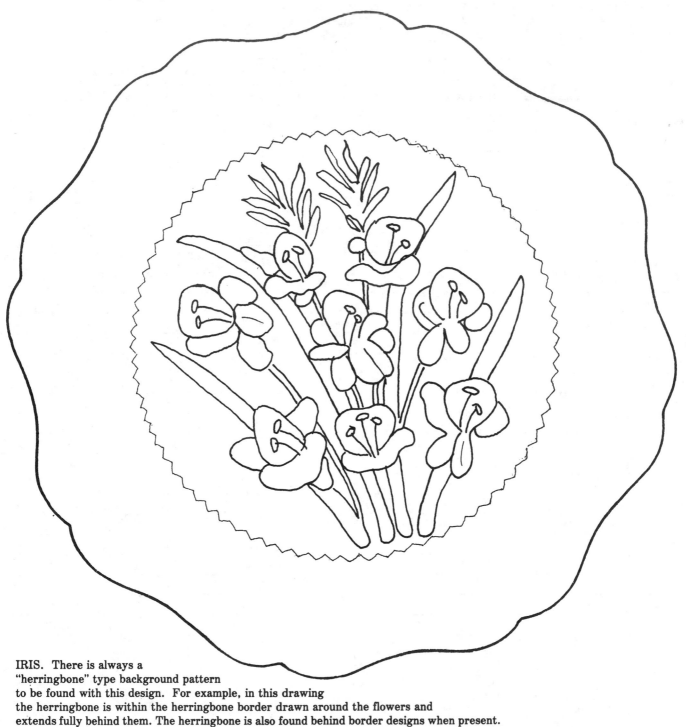

IRIS.  There is always a
"herringbone" type background pattern
to be found with this design.  For example, in this drawing
the herringbone is within the herringbone border drawn around the flowers and
extends fully behind them. The herringbone is also found behind border designs when present.

Colors found to date:

• Amber (iridescent)　　　• Blue　　　• Crystal　　　• Pink

# IRIS

## Reproductions or reissues

There were some iridescent pieces of Iris issued in 1950 and 1969. Whether to call these reissues is a hazy proposition, but the production of crystal in 1969 can be called reissue, as well as a candy dish (no lid) released in 1970 in white. Reissues of the vases can be identified by the iridescent color and the candy dish reissue has no design on the bottom as the old ones do. These are the most recent reissues.

## General pattern notes

The 1928-32 original releases were in crystal with some odd pieces in pink. Note the design drawing on the previous page does not illustrate the fine line herringbone background that is always present.

The 7-1/2-inch soup bowl in crystal has become quite scarce and is considered fairly rare these days.

Coasters are quite rare and some items have appeared frosted.

| ITEM & DESCRIPTION | DOLLAR VALUE RANGES BY COLOR | |
| --- | --- | --- |
| | Crystal | Iridescent (amber) |
| Bowl, 4-1/2" (beaded edge) | 50-55 | 12-15 |
| Bowl, 5" | 100-125 | — |
| Bowl, 5" (ruffled edge) | 10-12 | 20-24 |
| Bowl, 7-1/2" | 145-165 | 60-65 |
| Bowl, 8" (beaded edge) | 85-95 | 30-35 |
| Bowl, 9-1/2" (ruffled) | 12-15 | 10-12 |
| Bowl, 11" (ruffled edge) | 12-15 | 10-12 |
| Bowl, 11" | 85-95 | — |
| Butter dish and cover | 60-65 | 40-45 |
| Candlesticks (pair) | 40-45 | 37-43 |
| Candy jar and cover | 175-195 | — |
| Coaster | 110-115 | — |
| Creamer (footed) | 12-15 | 12-15 |
| Cup | 12-15 | 12-15 |
| Demitasse cup | 40-45 | 145-160 |
| Demitasse saucer | 125-145 | 200-225 |
| Fruit or nut set | 125-145 | 125-145 |
| Goblet, 4" | — | 28-30 |
| Goblet, 4-1/2" | 20-24 | — |
| Goblet, 5-3/4" (two styles) | 28-30 | 195-220 |
| Pitcher, 9-1/2" (footed) | 35-40 | 40-45 |
| Plate, 5-1/2" | 15-18 | 12-14 |
| Plate, 8" | 95-110 | — |
| Plate, 9" | 55-60 | 45-50 |
| Plate, 11-3/4" | 30-35 | 30-35 |
| Saucer | 8-10 | 8-10 |
| Sherbet, 2-1/2" (footed) | 25-28 | 12-15 |
| Sherbet, 4" (footed) | 25-28 | 200-225 |
| Sugar and cover | 28-30 | 24-28 |
| Tumbler, 4" | 125-145 | — |
| Tumbler, 6" (footed) | 18-20 | 16-18 |
| Tumbler, 6-1/2" (footed) | 30-35 | — |
| Vase, 9" | 28-30 | 24-28 |

# JUBILEE

1920 s-1930 s

Lancaster Glass Company

Lancaster, Ohio

# JUBILEE

**Reproductions or reissues**

None known to date.

**General pattern notes**

Although there are no reproductions or reissues in this pattern, there are several very similar pieces to be found. The principal differences are that the similar patterns have alternating large small petals and the centers of the flowers frequently have design detail, while Jubilee has void centers and the petals are more uniform in size. The designs are otherwise so similar that the non-Jubilee items mix and match well.

The pattern color is predominantly yellow, but very few pieces have been found in pink.

The rarest item to be found is the three-piece mayonnaise set consisting of plate, bowl, and serving spoon. The spoon is seldom found.

| ITEM & DESCRIPTION | DOLLAR VALUE RANGES BY COLOR |
| --- | --- |
| | Yellow |
| Bowl, 9" (handled) | 100-125 |
| Candle holder (pair) | 165-185 |
| Cheese and cracker set | 225-245 |
| Creamer | 18-20 |
| Sugar | 18-20 |
| Cup | 14-16 |
| Saucer | 3-5 |
| Goblet, 7 oz., 5-1/2" | 95-110 |
| Goblet, 11 oz., 7-1/2" | 165-185 |
| Mayonnaise set (three pieces), | 275-295 |
| without the serving spoon | 225-245 |
| Plate, 7" | 12-14 |
| Plate, 8-3/4" | 12-14 |
| Plate, 13" (handled) | 45-50 |
| Sherbet, 4-3/4" | 65-75 |
| Tray, 11" (two-handled) | 45-50 |
| Tray (center handled) | 220-225 |

# LACE EDGE
## 1935 - 1938

Hocking Glass Company                    (now Anchor-Hocking Glass Corporation)

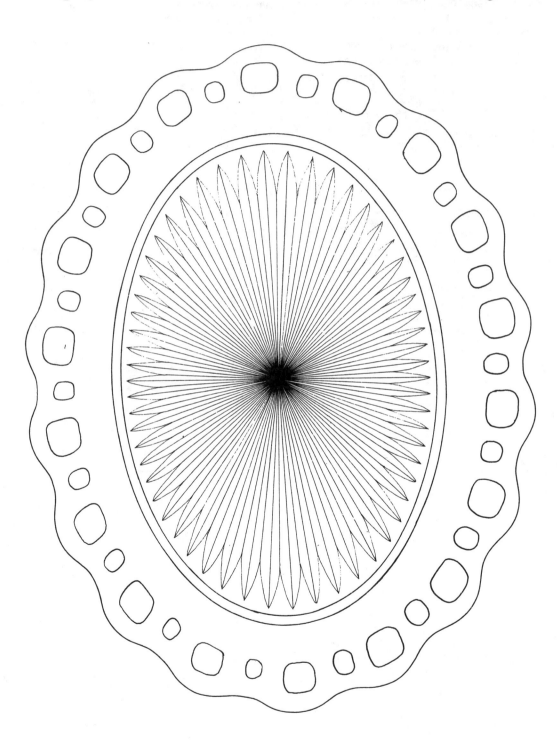

**Colors found to date:**

- Crystal                              - Pink

# LACE EDGE

**Reproductions or reissues**

None known to date.

**General pattern notes**

The characteristic lace edge of this pattern is not utilized on cups, creamers, sugars, or tumblers.

Hocking made this pattern mostly in pink, with just a few in crystal. Other companies made items much like Lace Edge in other colors, so don't confuse them.

Hocking also made some of these pieces in a "frosted" or "satin" finish. These are worth only about 50-percent of those listed below.

| ITEM & DESCRIPTION | DOLLAR VALUE RANGES BY COLOR |
|---|---|
| | Pink |
| Bowl, 6-3/8" | 26-28 |
| Bowl, 7-3/4" | 50-60 |
| Bowl, 9-1/2" (plain or ribbed) | 28-30 |
| Bowl, 10-1/2" (three-legged) | 225-250 |
| Butter dish or bon bon dish with cover | 85-95 |
| Candlesticks (pair) | 275-295 |
| Candy jar and cover (ribbed) | 85-95 |
| Compote, 7" (footed) | 30-35 |
| Compote and cover (footed) | 70-80 |
| Cookie jar and cover | 95-115 |
| Creamer | 25-35 |
| Cup | 28-30 |
| Fish bowl, 1/2 gal., 1 gal., 2 gal., (crystal only: 35-40) | — |
| Flower bowl (with crystal frog) | 45-50 |
| Plate, 7-1/4" | 30-35 |
| Plate, 8-3/4" | 25-28 |
| Plate, 10-1/2" | 36-38 |
| Plate, 10-1/2" (grill) | 24-26 |
| Plate, 10-1/2" relish (three sections) | 28-30 |
| Plate, 13" (solid lace, four sections) | 60-65 |
| Platter, 12-3/4" | 46-48 |
| Platter, 12-3/4" (five sections) | 42-45 |
| Relish dish, 7-1/2" (three sections) | 65-75 |
| Saucer | 12-14 |
| Sherbet (footed) | 125-145 |
| Sugar | 35-45 |
| Tumbler, 3-1/2" | 145-165 |
| Tumbler, 4-1/2" | 28-30 |
| Tumbler, 5" | 85-95 |
| Vase, 7" | 700-800 |

# LINCOLN INN

### c. 1930

Fenton Art Glass Company                                Williamstown, West Virginia

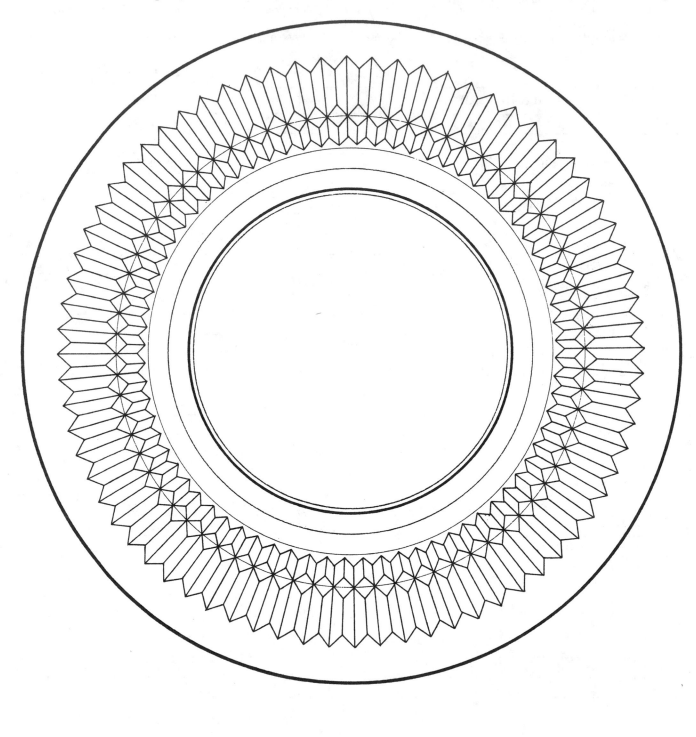

Colors in this pattern:

- Amethyst        • Aquamarine        • Black        • Blue
- Cobalt or Royal Blue        • Crystal        • Green        • Jade (translucent)
- Pink        • Red        • Yellow

# LINCOLN INN

## Reproductions or reissues
None known to date.

## General pattern notes
Advertising indicates the first release of this pattern by Fenton was in 1928. Colors noted on the previous page may or may not have been found. They are taken from several references and from old Fenton advertising.

This is fine quality glass, much of it handmade. It is not, strictly speaking, Depression glass, but it is of the same era.

Salt and pepper shakers seem to be the most elusive pieces in the pattern.

| ITEM & DESCRIPTION | DOLLAR VALUE RANGES BY COLOR | |
| --- | --- | --- |
| | Blue or Red | Other Colors |
| Ashtray | — | 8-10 |
| Bon bon (square) | 20-24 | 16-18 |
| Bon bon (oval) | 20-24 | 16-18 |
| Bowl, 5" | 20-24 | 12-16 |
| Bowl, 6" | 24-26 | 18-20 |
| Bowl, 6" (crimped edge) | 24-28 | 16-18 |
| Bowl, olive (with handle) | 24-28 | 14-18 |
| Bowl, finger | 30-36 | 15-20 |
| Bowl, 9-1/4" (footed) | — | 35-40 |
| Bowl, 10-1/2" (footed) | 85-95 | 40-50 |
| Candy dish (footed, oval) | 40-50 | 15-30 |
| Compote | 40-50 | 12-16 |
| Creamer | 25-30 | 14-20 |
| Cup | 20-24 | 12-18 |
| Goblet, water | 35-40 | 20-30 |
| Goblet, wine | 30-35 | 15-20 |
| Nut dish (footed) | 40-50 | 18-35 |
| Pitcher, 7-1/4" | 650-750 | 400-500 |
| Plate, 6" | 10-12 | 6-8 |
| Plate, 8" | 20-25 | 10-15 |
| Plate, 9-1/4" | 40-50 | 24-30 |
| Plate, 12" | 40-50 | 24-30 |
| Salt and pepper (pair) | 350-450 | 195-225 |
| Saucer | 5-6 | 3-4 |
| Sherbet, 4-3/4" | 25-30 | 15-20 |
| Sugar | 25-30 | 12-15 |
| Tumbler, 4 oz. | 25-30 | 14-18 |
| Tumbler, 5 oz. (footed) | 30-35 | 15-20 |
| Tumbler, 7 oz. (footed) | 32-38 | 15-20 |
| Tumbler, 9 oz. (footed) | 35-40 | 16-20 |
| Tumbler, 12 oz. (footed) | 45-50 | 25-35 |
| Vase, 12" (footed) | 150-175 | — |

# LORAIN
## 1929 - 1932

Indiana Glass Company                                    Dunkirk, Indiana

Colors found to date:

• Crystal          • Green          • Yellow

# LORAIN (No. 615)

**Reproductions or reissues**

None known to date.

**General pattern notes**

Yellow is the most frequently found color, but difficult to obtain insofar as a complete set is concerned.

One of the rarer items to be found is the 10-1/4-inch dinner plate in yellow and the larger dinner plates are thought to be non-existent. Rarer still is the deep 8-inch bowl.

The pattern is sometimes known as "Basket."

| ITEM & DESCRIPTION | DOLLAR VALUE RANGES BY COLOR | |
|---|---|---|
| | Crystal or Green | Yellow |
| Bowl, 6" | 35-50 | 60-65 |
| Bowl, 7-1/4" | 35-50 | 60-65 |
| Bowl, 8" | 100-125 | 145-165 |
| Bowl, 9-3/4" (oval) | 35-50 | 60-65 |
| Creamer (footed) | 14-20 | 24-26 |
| Cup | 12-15 | 14-16 |
| Plate, 5-1/2" | 6-10 | 12-14 |
| Plate, 7-3/4" | 6-10 | 12-14 |
| Plate, 8-3/8" | 14-20 | 28-30 |
| Plate, 10-1/4" | 45-60 | 85-95 |
| Platter, 11-1/2" | 20-35 | 50-55 |
| Relish, 8" (four sections) | 18-26 | 35-40 |
| Saucer | 3-5 | 6-8 |
| Sherbet (footed) | 18-26 | 30-35 |
| Snack tray | 18-26 | — |
| Sugar (footed) | 14-20 | 24-26 |
| Tumbler, 4-3/4" (footed) | 18-26 | 30-35 |

# MADRID
## 1932 - 1939

Federal Glass Company                                    Columbus, Ohio

**Colors found to date:**

- Amber
- Green
- Blue
- Pink
- Crystal

# MADRID

## Reproductions or reissues

Madrid has been reissued twice—once by Federal and later by another company.

The first reissue was by Federal in communication of the Bicentennial and easily identified by the presence of a small "76" molded into the back of each piece. All these were issued in amber. There are a total of 14 pieces in this Bicentennial set. The amber color is darker than that on the old original issue.

There have been a few butter-dish tops to appear in crystal, some with the "76" and some without it. These were probably a trial run, so they are limited.

In 1982, the Indiana Glass Company, which had bought Federal's molds, reissued practically the entire line in crystal.

## General pattern notes

The first color this pattern was made in was green, followed a year or so later with amber.

The green was phased out and amber became the predominant color in which the pattern was made. Blue and pink were added, but neither color remained in production long.

The larger size pitchers in crystal, amber, and green are highly sought items, but the prize is the lazy Susan in wood, with the seven hot-plate coasters fitted.

Cups are found with the ribbing inside or out.

| ITEM & DESCRIPTION | DOLLAR VALUE RANGES BY COLOR | | | | |
|---|---|---|---|---|---|
| | Blue | Crystal | Amber | Green | Pink |
| Ashtray (square) | — | 97-110 | 195-220 | 175-195 | — |
| Bowl, 4-3/4" (cream soup) | — | 9-10 | 18-20 | — | — |
| Bowl, 5" | 28-30 | 4-5 | 8-10 | 8-10 | 8-10 |
| Bowl, 7" | 30-35 | 9-10 | 18-20 | 16-18 | — |
| Bowl, 8" | 45-50 | 7-8 | 14-16 | 18-20 | — |
| Bowl, 9-3/8" | — | 10-12 | 20-24 | — | 18-20 |
| Bowl, 9-1/2" | — | 17-20 | 35-40 | — | — |
| Bowl, 10" (oval) | 35-40 | 7-9 | 15-18 | 24-26 | 11-13 |
| Bowl, 11" (low console) | — | 9-10 | 18-20 | — | 12-14 |
| Butter dish and cover | — | 35-40 | 75-85 | — | 85-95 |
| Candlesticks, 2-1/4" (pair) | — | 13-14 | 26-28 | — | 26-28 |
| Cookie jar and cover | — | 20-22 | 40-45 | — | 28-30 |
| Creamer (footed) | 22-24 | 3-4 | 6-8 | 9-10 | — |
| Cup | 18-20 | 3-5 | 6-10 | 7-11 | 12-14 |
| Gravy boat and drip plate | — | 1,200-1,300 | 2,400-2,600 | — | — |
| Hot dish coaster | — | 40-45 | 85-95 | 85-95 | — |
| Jam dish, 7" | 40-45 | 14-15 | 28-30 | 20-24 | — |
| Jell-O Mold, 2-1/8" | — | 8-9 | 16-18 | — | — |
| Pitcher, 5-1/2" | — | 20-25 | 45-50 | — | — |
| Pitcher, 8" | 195-225 | 20-25 | 25-50 | 145-160 | 30-35 |
| Pitcher, 8-1/2" | — | 35-40 | 75-85 | 225-250 | — |
| Pitcher, 8-1/2" (ice lip) | — | 35-40 | 75-85 | 225-250 | — |
| Plate, 6" | 6-8 | 2-3 | 4-5 | 4-5 | 3-4 |
| Plate, 7-1/2" | 18-20 | 3-4 | 6-8 | 8-10 | 6-8 |
| Plate, 8-7/8" | 18-20 | 3-4 | 6-8 | 8-10 | 6-8 |
| Plate, 10-1/2" | 75-85 | 25-30 | 55-60 | 50-55 | — |
| Plate, 10-1/2" (grill) | — | 5-6 | 10-12 | 18-20 | — |
| Plate, 10-1/4" (relish) | — | 8-9 | 16-18 | 16-18 | 12-14 |
| Plate, 11-1/4" (cake) | — | 9-10 | 18-20 | — | 12-14 |
| Platter, 11-1/2" (oval) | 28-30 | 9-10 | 18-20 | 18-20 | 12-16 |

| ITEM & DESCRIPTION | DOLLAR VALUE RANGES BY COLOR | | | | |
|---|---|---|---|---|---|
| | Blue | Crystal | Amber | Green | Pink |
| Salt and pepper, 3-1/2" (footed) | 165-175 | | 65-70 | 135-145 | 110-125 |
| Salt and pepper, 3-1/2" | — | 20-25 | 45-50 | 65-70 | — |
| Saucer | 8-10 | | 1-2 | 3-5 | 3-5 |
| Sherbet (two styles) | 18-20 | | 3-4 | 6-8 | 10-12 |
| Sugar and cover | 235-245 | | 25-30 | 50-60 | 65-70 |
| Tumbler, 3-7/8" | 40-45 | | 7-8 | 14-16 | 30-35 |
| Tumbler, 4-1/4" | 30-35 | | 7-8 | 14-16 | 18-20 |
| Tumbler, 5-1/2" | 40-45 | | 11-12 | 22-24 | 28-30 |
| Tumbler, 4" (footed) | — | 14-15 | 28-30 | 40-45 | — |
| Tumbler, 5-1/2" (footed) | — | 15-16 | 30-35 | 45-50 | — |
| Wooden lazy Susan, with seven small hot-dish coasters | — | — | 600-700 | 1,200-1,500 | — |

# MANHATTAN

## 1938 - 1941

### Anchor-Hocking Glass Corporation

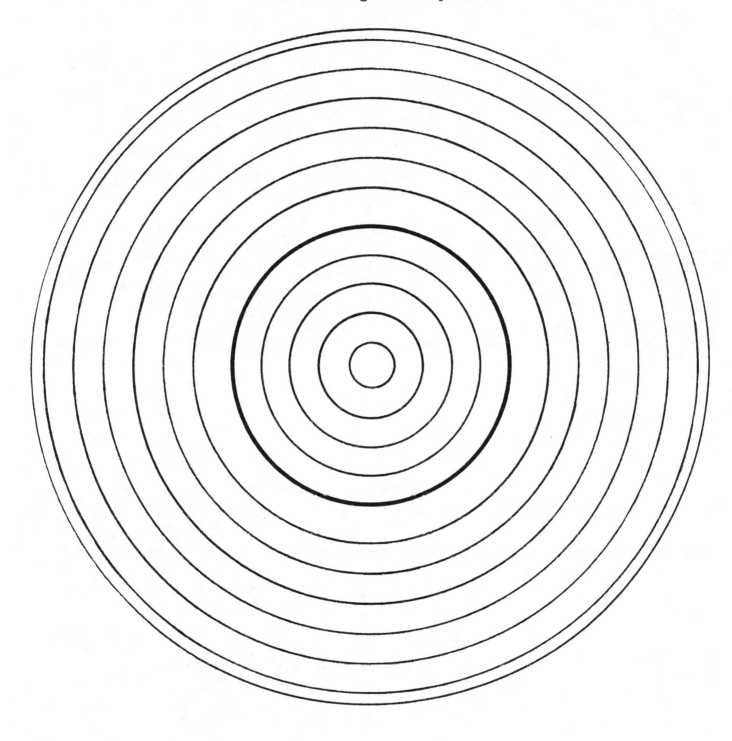

**Colors found to date:**

- Crystal
- Green
- Pink
- Red (Ruby Red)

# MANHATTAN

**Reproductions or reissues**

None known to date.

**General pattern notes**

The green seems to edge out the other colors in amount available. The ruby red and pink are not often seen and the crystal, which follows pink in availability, was introduced in 1940.

One of the most popular items in this pattern line is the five-section relish tray with contrasting colored inserts. The round tilted pitcher remains a favorite also.

| ITEM & DESCRIPTION | DOLLAR VALUE RANGES BY COLOR | |
| --- | --- | --- |
| | Crystal | Pink |
| Ashtray | 14-16 | — |
| Bowl, 4-1/2" | 8-10 | — |
| Bowl, 5-3/8" (handled) | 16-18 | 18-20 |
| Bowl, 7-1/2" | 18-20 | — |
| Bowl, 8" (closed handles) | 20-24 | 26-28 |
| Bowl, 9" | 24-26 | — |
| Bowl, 9-1/2" | 35-40 | 40-45 |
| Candlesticks, 4-1/2" (pair) | 16-18 | — |
| Candy dish (three legged) | — | 14-16 |
| Candy dish and cover | 38-40 | — |
| Coaster | 18-20 | — |
| Compote, 5-3/4" | 38-40 | 40-45 |
| Creamer | 10-12 | 14-16 |
| Cup | 18-20 | 175-195 |
| Relish tray, 14" (four sections) | 24-28 | 30-35 |
| Relish tray, 14" (five sections) | 24-28 | 30-35 |
| Relish tray insert | 6-8 | 8-10 |
| Pitcher, 24 oz. | 30-35 | — |
| Pitcher, 80 oz. (tilted) | 45-50 | 65-75 |
| Plate, 6" | 8-10 | 65-75 |
| Plate, 8-1/2" | 18-20 | 7-10 |
| Plate, 10-1/4" | 24-26 | 200-225 |
| Plate, 14" | 30-35 | — |
| Salt and pepper, 2" (pair) | 35-40 | 65-75 |
| Saucer | 5-6 | 65-75 |
| Sherbet | 10-12 | 20-24 |
| Sugar | 10-12 | 14-16 |
| Tumbler, 10 oz. (footed) | 18-20 | 22-24 |
| Vase, 8" | 25-30 | — |
| Wine glass | 4-6 | — |

# MAYFAIR

1934

Federal Glass Company

Columbus, Ohio

Colors found to date:

- Amber          • Crystal          • Green

# MAYFAIR

**Reproductions or reissues**

None known to date.

**General pattern notes**

A pattern which is in short supply, Mayfair was discontinued soon after production began. It seems that Federal tried to register the name with its design copyright, only to find out that the "Mayfair" name had already been registered to another company. Subsequently, it removed it from production. After some experimentation with design changes, they had reworked the molds to the "Rosemary" design. The resulting design transition pieces are usually lumped in with one or the other, but they are really neither. Interesting they are, but should be considered oddities, the collection of which is entirely up to the collector's disposition.

| ITEM & DESCRIPTION | DOLLAR VALUE RANGES BY COLOR | | |
| --- | --- | --- | --- |
| | Amber | Crystal | Green |
| Bowl, 5" | 8-10 | 5-6 | 10-12 |
| Bowl, 5" (cream soup) | 18-20 | 8-10 | 20-22 |
| Bowl, 6" | 15-18 | 6-8 | 18-20 |
| Bowl, 10" (oval) | 25-28 | 10-12 | 30-35 |
| Creamer (footed) | 12-15 | 4-5 | 16-18 |
| Cup | 8-10 | 4-5 | 8-10 |
| Plate, 6-3/4" | 8-10 | 4-5 | 8-10 |
| Plate, 9-1/2" | 12-15 | 8-10 | 12-15 |
| Plate, 9-1/2" (grill) | 10-12 | 8-10 | 10-12 |
| Platter, 12" (oval) | 28-30 | 12-14 | 30-35 |
| Saucer | 3-4 | 1-2 | 3-4 |
| Sugar (footed) | 12-15 | 4-5 | 16-18 |
| Tumbler, 4-1/2" | 28-30 | 12-14 | 30-35 |

# MAYFAIR (OPEN ROSE)

**1931 - 1937**

**Hocking Glass Company**                    (Now Anchor-Hocking Glass Corporation)

**Colors found to date:**

- Blue
- Crystal
- Green
- Pink
- Yellow

# MAYFAIR (OPEN ROSE)

## Reproductions or reissues

Until recently, it was thought there were reproductions of only the whiskey jiggers. They first surfaced in 1978 and can be found in pink, green, and blue. The identification of the reproduction jigger in green and blue is easy, for the original was not made in either color. The pink might cause you some trouble if you can't compare with a known original. It has been reported that the reproductions all have incomplete pattern design and their bases are thicker.

There are now reproductions of the salt and pepper shakers and the cookie jar.

## General pattern notes

This is the "Mayfair" pattern that resulted in Federal discontinuing its own Mayfair pattern when it discovered that Hocking had already registered the name. There is no similarity of design.

Also called "Open Rose" by some, this is one of the most popularly collected patterns of Depression era glassware.

Mayfair was originally released in pink. The original line had more than 50 items in it. Soon after came the blue and some pieces of green. Only a very modest number of pieces were made in crystal and along with the scarcity of crystal goes yellow.

Rarest of the pieces in this collection are the three-leg nine-inch bowl, the pair of footed salt and pepper shakers, both in pink, and pink-, green-, or yellow-footed sugars with lid. Whiskey jiggers appear in pink only. There are some items that have been found with a frosted finish and the flower mold design around the border has been painted in realistic colors. There are several others that will require the extraction of a tooth or two in terms of money required for acquisition. See the following value list. Perhaps you'll get lucky and find some in Aunt Minnie's cellar.

| ITEM & DESCRIPTION | DOLLAR VALUE RANGES BY COLOR | | | |
|---|---|---|---|---|
| | Blue | Green | Pink | Yellow |
| Bowl, 5" (cream soup) | — | — | 50-55 | — |
| Bowl, 5-1/2" | 55-60 | 85-95 | 28-30 | 75-85 |
| Bowl, 7" | 50-55 | 135-145 | 35-40 | 145-155 |
| Bowl, 9" (console, three-legged) | — | 4,800-5,000 | 4,800-5,000 | — |
| Bowl, 9-1/2" (oval) | 75-80 | 125-145 | 34-38 | 140-150 |
| Bowl, 10" | 75-80 | — | 30-35 | 145-155 |
| Bowl, 10" (covered) | 175-185 | — | 125-135 | 900-1000 |
| Bowl, 11-3/4" | 70-80 | 65-75 | 60-70 | 200-225 |
| Bowl, 12" (scalloped edge) | 100-115 | 60-70 | 60-70 | 225-250 |
| Butter dish and cover | 300-325 | 1,300-1,400 | 100-125 | 1,300-1,400 |
| Cake plate, 10" (footed) | 75-85 | 100-125 | 40-45 | — |
| Candy dish and cover | 325-345 | 600-650 | 65-75 | 550-600 |
| Celery dish, 9" (sectioned) | — | 185-195 | 185-195 | 185-195 |
| Celery dish, 10" (plain or sectioned) | 65-75 | 125-145 | 50-250 | 125-150 |
| Cookie jar and cover | 300-325 | 650-700 | 60-70 | 850-950 |
| Creamer | 70-80 | 200-225 | 30-35 | 225-245 |
| Cup (square shape) | 50-60 | 150-160 | 18-20 | 160-170 |
| Decanter with stopper | — | — | 215-225 | — |
| Goblet, 3-3/4" | — | 950-1050 | 1,200-1,300 | — |
| Goblet, 4", 2-1/2 oz. | — | 900-1000 | 900-1000 | — |
| Goblet, 4", 3-1/2 oz. | — | 350-400 | 95-100 | — |
| Goblet, 4-1/2" | — | 400-450 | 100-125 | — |
| Goblet, 5-1/4" | 950-1,000 | — | 1,100-1,200 | — |
| Goblet, 5-3/4" | — | 495-525 | 75-85 | — |
| Goblet, 7-1/4" | 225-250 | — | 250-300 | — |
| Pitcher, 6" | 175-195 | 500-600 | 60-70 | 500-600 |
| Pitcher, 8" | 175-195 | 500-600 | 70-80 | 500-600 |
| Pitcher, 8-1/2" | 250-275 | 700-800 | 120-130 | 700-800 |

| ITEM & DESCRIPTION | DOLLAR VALUE RANGES BY COLOR | | | |
|---|---|---|---|---|
| | Blue | Green | Pink | Yellow |
| Plate, 6" | 20-24 | 75-85 | 10-12 | 85-95 |
| Plate, 6-1/2" | — | — | 16-18 | — |
| Plate, 6-1/2" (ringed off-center) | 45-50 | 125-150 | 30-35 | 135-145 |
| Plate, 8-1/2" | 50-60 | 85-95 | 28-30 | 135-145 |
| Plate, 9-1/2" | 85-95 | 150-175 | 50-60 | 145-155 |
| Plate, 9-1/2" (grill) | 50-60 | 85-95 | 45-50 | 85-95 |
| Plate, 11-1/2" (grill with handles) | — | — | — | 100-125 |
| Plate, 12" (cake, handled) | 75-85 | 60-70 | 60-70 | — |
| Platter, 12-1/2" (oval with open or closed handles) | | — | — | — |
| Relish, 8-3/8" (plain or four-sectioned) | 65-75 | — | 175-275 | 50-250 |
| Salt and pepper (pair) | 300-325 | — | 1,100-1,200 | 70-80 |
| Salt and pepper (footed) | — | — | 7,000-8,000 | — |
| Sandwich server (center handled) | 85-95 | | 60-70 | 55-60 |
| Saucer (ringed) | — | — | 35-40 | — |
| Saucer | 20-24 | — | 75-85 | 10-12 |
| Sherbet, 2-1/4" | 145-155 | — | — | 165-175 |
| Sherbet, 3" (footed) | — | — | 20-24 | — |
| Sherbet, 4-3/4" (footed) | 85-95 | — | 160-170 | 85-95 |
| Sugar | 70-80 | — | 200-225 | 30-35 |
| Sugar cover | — | 1,000-1,200 | | 1,200-1,400 |
| Tumbler, 3-1/2" | 125-135 | — | — | 40-50 |
| Tumbler, 4-1/4" | 110-125 | — | — | 35-45 |
| Tumbler, 4-3/4" | 135-145 | — | 200-225 | 200-225 |
| Tumbler, 5-1/4" | 275-300 | — | — | 60-65 |
| Tumbler, 3-1/4" (footed) | — | — | 85-95 | — |
| Tumbler, 5-1/4" (footed) | 125-145 | — | 50-60 | 195-205 |
| Tumbler, 6-1/2" (footed) | 275-295 | 245-260 | 50-60 | — |
| Vase | 125-145 | 300-350 | 175-195 | — |
| Whiskey jigger, 2-1/4", 1-1/2 oz. | — | — | 75-85 | — |

# MISS AMERICA
## 1933 - 1937

Hocking Glass Company                    (now Anchor-Hocking Glass Corporation)

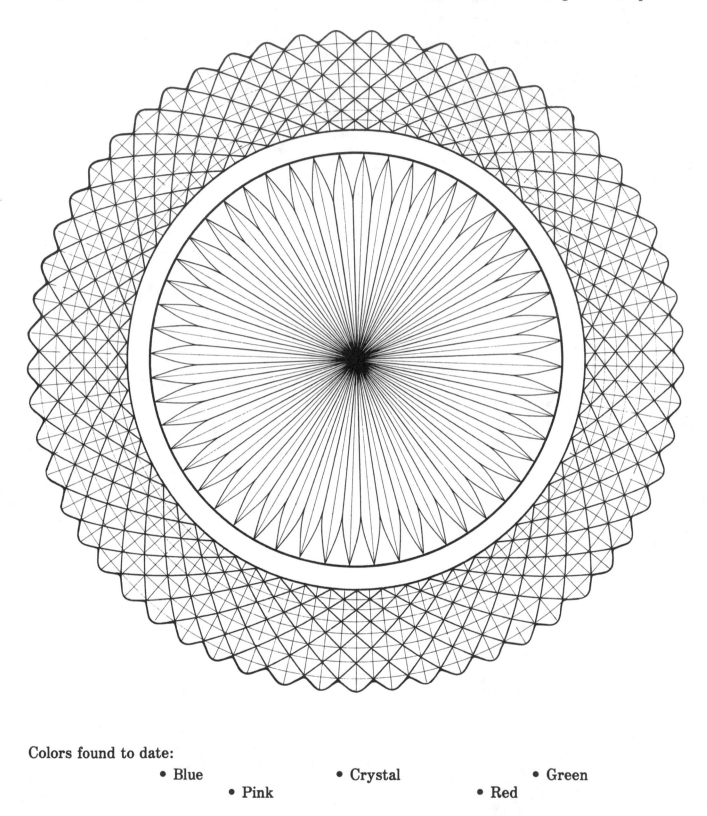

Colors found to date:

- Blue
- Crystal
- Green
- Pink
- Red

# MISS AMERICA

## Reproductions or reissues

Covered butter dishes and salt and pepper shakers have been reproduced in Miss America in crystal, blue, green, pink, and amber. A physical comparison is the best way to tell the difference between old and new, but if that is not practical, the cover presents the best evidence. If you invert the cover and feel inside just beneath the knob and can discern a definite round protrusion, you have an original. The new covers don't exhibit this rounded protrusion. Also, if you hold the old one up to a light and look from inside, outward through the knob, you will see a distinct geometrical star. If you look at the new cover the same way, the star is there, but it is uneven with indistinct points.

The reproduction salt and pepper shakers are crude, hobs don't have the sharp feel of the original and the lower portion next to the square base seems filled with glass. The inside depth of the old is about one-half inch deeper than the reproduction. The colors of the reproductions are crystal, green, and pink.

Pitchers and tumblers have been reproduced. The new tumblers have twice as thick bottoms as the originals. The handles on the old are just below a hump on the rim of the pitcher top. New ones have no hump.

## General pattern notes

New collectors have a tendency to confuse "Miss America" with "English Hobnail." Turn back to Page 64 and read the discussion of the differences.

Red is the color to look for in Miss America. Any piece in red is a real prize. Pink and crystal are the most commonly found and collected colors.

Of the rare pieces, the butter dish and cover intact, as well as the shakers, 8-inch and 8-1/2-inch pitchers, and pink goblets are all quite desirable.

| ITEM & DESCRIPTION | DOLLAR VALUE RANGES BY COLOR | | | |
| --- | --- | --- | --- | --- |
| | Crystal | Green | Pink | Red |
| Bowl, 4-1/2" | — | — | — | — |
| Bowl, 6-1/4" | 8-10 | 18-20 | 30-35 | — |
| Bowl, 8" | 45-50 | — | 90-100 | 450-550 |
| Bowl, 8-3/4" | 45-50 | — | 80-90 | — |
| Bowl, 10" (oval) | 14-16 | — | 65-75 | — |
| Butter dish and cover | 250-275 | — | 650-700 | — |
| Cake plate, 12" (footed) | 25-30 | — | 65-75 | — |
| Candy jar and cover, 11-1/2" | 75-85 | — | 160-175 | — |
| Celery dish, 10-1/2" | 14-16 | — | 35-40 | — |
| Coaster, 5-3/4" | 18-20 | — | 35-45 | — |
| Compote, 5" | 18-20 | — | 35-45 | — |
| Creamer (footed) | 10-12 | — | 24-26 | 200-250 |
| Cup | 10-12 | 18-20 | 24-26 | 250-300 |
| Goblet, 3-3/4" | 24-26 | — | 100-110 | 300-350 |
| Goblet, 4-3/4" | 26-28 | — | 110-125 | 300-350 |
| Goblet, 5-1/2" | 20-22 | — | 65-75 | 300-350 |
| Pitcher, 8" | 60-70 | — | 150-175 | — |
| Pitcher, 8-1/2" | 70-80 | — | 250-275 | — |
| Plate, 5-3/4" | 6-8 | 8-10 | 8-10 | 50-60 |
| Plate, 6-3/4" | — | 10-12 | — | — |
| Plate, 8-1/2" | 8-10 | 10-12 | — | 150-175 |
| Plate, 10-1/4" | 18-20 | — | 40-45 | — |
| Plate, 10-1/4" (grill) | 12-15 | — | 30-35 | — |
| Platter, 12-1/4" (oval) | 18-20 | — | 50-60 | — |
| Relish, 8-3/4" (4 sections) | 14-16 | — | 26-28 | — |
| Relish, 11-3/4" (sectioned, round) | 40-45 | — | 3,000-5,000 | — |
| Salt and pepper (pair) | 35-40 | 400-450 | 75-85 | — |

| ITEM & DESCRIPTION | DOLLAR VALUE RANGES BY COLOR | | | |
|---|---|---|---|---|
| | Crystal | Green | Pink | Red |
| Saucer | 4-6 | — | 8-10 | 65-75 |
| Sherbet | 8-10 | — | 18-20 | 150-175 |
| Sugar | 10-12 | — | 24-26 | 200-250 |
| Tumbler, 4" | 18-20 | — | 65-75 | — |
| Tumbler, 4-1/2" | 18-20 | 25-30 | 60-70 | — |
| Tumbler, 6-3/4" | 30-35 | — | 100-125 | — |

# MODERNTONE

1934 - late 1940 s

Hazel Atlas Glass Company

Clarksburg, West Virginia and Zanesville, Ohio

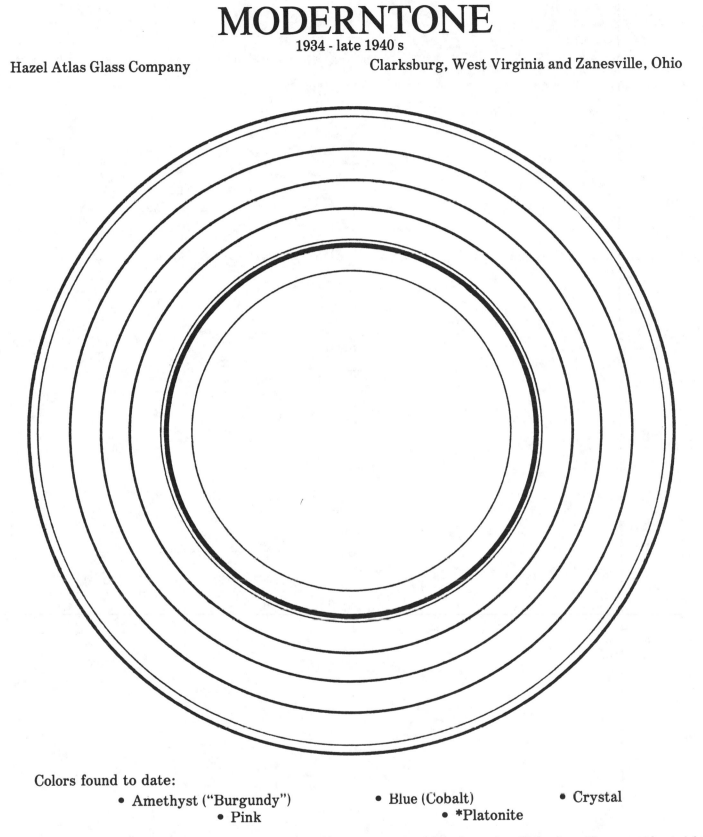

Colors found to date:

- Amethyst ("Burgundy")
- Pink
- Blue (Cobalt)
- *Platonite
- Crystal

*Platonite was a heat resistant opaque coating that was applied to the pieces and fired onto them like a glaze. There are at least eight different colors to be found.

# MODERNTONE

**Reproductions or reissues**

None known to date.

**General pattern notes**

Moderntone is also called "Wedding Band" and has a very simple, but attractive, design. Moderntone is found mostly in the cobalt blue. Very few pieces are found in pink or crystal. At present, they are not particularly sought, for it is believed that there weren't enough pieces made in those colors to warrant collecting them. Blue and amethyst 7-1/2-inch bowls are practically impossible to find. The butter dish and cheese dishes, each with metal covers, and the ashtrays would make a collector jump for joy if they were to pick them up as bargains at flea markets or yard sales.

| ITEM & DESCRIPTION | DOLLAR VALUE RANGES BY COLOR | |
| --- | --- | --- |
| | Amethyst | Blue (Cobalt) |
| Ashtray | — | 165-175 |
| Bowl, 4-3/4" (cream soup) | 18-20 | 20-24 |
| Bowl, 5" | 28-30 | 32-35 |
| Bowl, 5" (cream soup, ruffled edge) | 40-45 | 75-85 |
| Bowl, 6-1/2" | 75-85 | 85-95 |
| Bowl, 7-1/2" | 100-125 | 150-175 |
| Bowl, 8-3/4" | 45-50 | 50-60 |
| Butter dish and metal cover | — | 125-150 |
| Cheese dish and metal cover, 7" | — | 450-495 |
| Creamer | 10-12 | 12-14 |
| Cup | 10-12 | 12-14 |
| Cup | 16-18 | 20-24 |
| Plate, 5-3/4" | 5-6 | 6-8 |
| Plate, 6-3/4" | 8-10 | 12-15 |
| Plate, 7-3/4" | 8-10 | 12-15 |
| Plate, 8-7/8" | 14-16 | 18-20 |
| Plate, 10-1/2" | 45-50 | 65-75 |
| Platter, 11" (oval) | 40-45 | 50-60 |
| Platter, 12" (oval) | 60-70 | 85-95 |
| Salt and pepper (pair) | 45-50 | 50-60 |
| Saucer | 4-5 | 5-6 |
| Sherbet | 12-14 | 16-18 |
| Sugar and metal cover | 16-18 | 45-50 |
| Tumbler, 9 oz. | 30-35 | 38-40 |
| Whiskey jigger, 1-1/2 oz. | — | 45-50 |

# MOONSTONE
## 1941-1946
## Anchor-Hocking Glass Corporation

### Colors found to date
Crystal with white opalescent highlights; green with opalescent highlights.

### Reproductions or reissues
None known to date.

### General pattern notes
There is no pattern drawing with this listing, for the pattern design is virtually the same as that of "Hobnail" on Page 92. The difference is that the hobs and edges of the glass in Moonstone are opalescent. Moonstone also has some rough-edge pieces.

Up until recently, it was thought that the opalescent white was the only color manufactured, but it is now known that green was also produced. The green is quite rare and presently too unique to value.

| ITEM & DESCRIPTION | DOLLAR VALUE RANGES BY COLOR |
|---|---|
| | Opalescent Hobnails |
| Bonbon (heart shaped) | 14-16 |
| Bowl, 5-1/2" | 14-16 |
| Bowl, 5-1/2" (ruffled) | 10-12 |
| Bowl, 6-1/2" (handled) | 8-10 |
| Bowl, 7-3/4" | 14-16 |
| Bowl, 7-3/4" (relish, sectioned) | 10-12 |
| Bowl, 9-1/2" | 20-24 |
| Bowl (cloverleaf shaped) | 11-14 |
| Candleholders (pair) | 18-20 |
| Candy jar and cover, 6" | 30-35 |
| Cigarette box and cover | 20-24 |
| Creamer | 8-10 |
| Cup | 6-8 |
| Goblet | 18-20 |
| Plate, 6-1/4" | 4-5 |
| Plate, 8" | 10-12 |
| Plate, 10" | 26-28 |
| Powder puff box and cover, 4-3/4" | 24-26 |
| Saucer | 3-4 |
| Sherbet (footed) | 6-8 |
| Sugar (footed) | 8-10 |
| Vase, bud | 16-18 |

# MT. PLEASANT or DOUBLE SHIELD

### c. 1930

L. E. Smith Glass Company

**MT. PLEASANT.**
This drawing is the bottom
side of a black 6½" piece.  The pattern
design does not appear on the upper surface.

**\*Colors found to date:**

- Black       • Blue       • Green       • Pink

\* Amber was mentioned in early catalogs.

# MOUNT PLEASANT or DOUBLE SHIELD

**Reproductions or reissues**

None known to date.

**General pattern notes**

There seems to be quite a variety of shapes in this pattern. Some would not appear to belong at first glance, but old catalogs illustrate them together as "Mt. Pleasant." There are round and square plates, the former with scalloped edges and the latter with scallops alternating with single and double points. Some pieces are found with gold handles and some with gold edge trim. There have been several black pieces found with sterling silver surface decorations. Most of these are worn off with heavy use and can be difficult to detect.

| ITEM & DESCRIPTION | DOLLAR VALUE RANGES BY COLOR | |
|---|---|---|
| | **Black or Blue** | **Green or Pink** |
| Bowl (three-legged) | 26-30 | 18-24 |
| Bowl, 8" (scalloped, two-handled) | 30-35 | 18-20 |
| Bowl, 8" (square, two-handled) | 30-35 | 18-20 |
| Candlesticks (single stem, pair) | 30-35 | 28-30 |
| Candlesticks (pair) | 45-50 | 30-35 |
| Creamer | 18-20 | 16-18 |
| Cup | 14-16 | 8-10 |
| Plate, 8" (two styles) | 14-16 | 10-12 |
| Plate, 8" (closed handles) | 18-20 | 12-14 |
| Plate, 10-1/2" (closed handles) | 34-36 | 14-16 |
| Salt and pepper (pair) | 50-60 | 30-35 |
| Saucer (two styles) | 4-5 | 3-4 |
| Sherbet | 16-18 | 10-12 |
| Sugar | 18-20 | 16-18 |

# NEW CENTURY
## C. 1930

Hazel Atlas Glass Company

Clarksburg, West Virginia and Zanesville Ohio

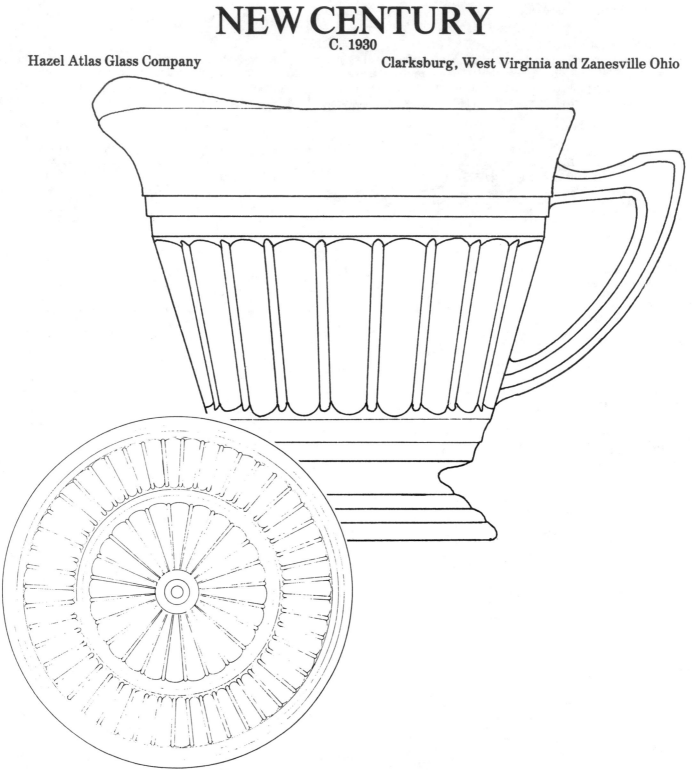

Flat pieces such as plates and the other items bear this alternating wide and narrow band pattern also and some of them exhibit radiated patterns out from two concentric circles or ovals as in lower illustration of a plate.

**Colors found to date:**

- Amethyst
- Crystal
- Black
- Green
- Blue (Cobalt)
- Pink

# NEW CENTURY

**Reproductions or reissues**

None known to date.

**General pattern notes**

Green is the predominant color in this pattern. Only a very few pieces have been found in other colors, with crystal leading the list as having been uncovered in the most different pieces.

Ashtrays and decanters are among the more scarce items in any color.

There have been reports of some fired-on opaque colors: red, blue, yellow, and green.

| | DOLLAR VALUE RANGES BY COLOR | |
|---|---|---|
| **ITEM & DESCRIPTION** | **Amethyst, Cobalt, or Pink** | **Crystal or Green** |
| Ashtray | — | 24-26 |
| Bowl, 4-1/2" | — | 16-18 |
| Bowl, 4-3/4" (cream soup) | — | 18-20 |
| Bowl, 8" | — | 22-24 |
| Bowl, 9" (covered casserole) | — | 65-75 |
| Butter dish and cover | — | 65-75 |
| Cup | 12-15 | 8-10 |
| Creamer | — | 8-10 |
| Decanter with stopper | — | 75-85 |
| Goblet, 2-1/2 oz. | — | 28-30 |
| Goblet, 3-1/4 oz. | — | 28-30 |
| Pitcher, 7-3/4" (two styles) | 35-40 | 35-40 |
| Pitcher, 8" (two styles) | 40-45 | 40-45 |
| Plate, 6" | — | 4-5 |
| Plate, 7-1/8" | — | 10-12 |
| Plate, 8-1/2" | — | 10-12 |
| Plate, 10" | — | 18-20 |
| Plate, 10" (grill) | — | 14-16 |
| Platter, 11" (oval) | — | 28-30 |
| Salt and pepper (shakers, pair) | — | 35-40 |
| Saucer | 6-8 | 4-5 |
| Sherbet, 3" | — | 8-10 |
| Sugar and cover | — | 24-28 |
| Tumbler, 3-1/2" | 14-16 | 14-16 |
| Tumbler, 4-1/8" | 14-16 | 14-16 |
| Tumbler, 5" | 18-20 | 18-20 |
| Tumbler, 5-1/4" | 28-30 | 28-30 |
| Tumbler, 4" (footed) | — | 26-28 |
| Tumbler, 4-7/8" (footed) | — | 26-28 |
| Whiskey jigger, 2-1/2" | — | 24-26 |

# NEWPORT

**1936 - 1940**

Hazel Atlas Glass Company

Clarksburg, West Virginia and Zanesville, Ohio

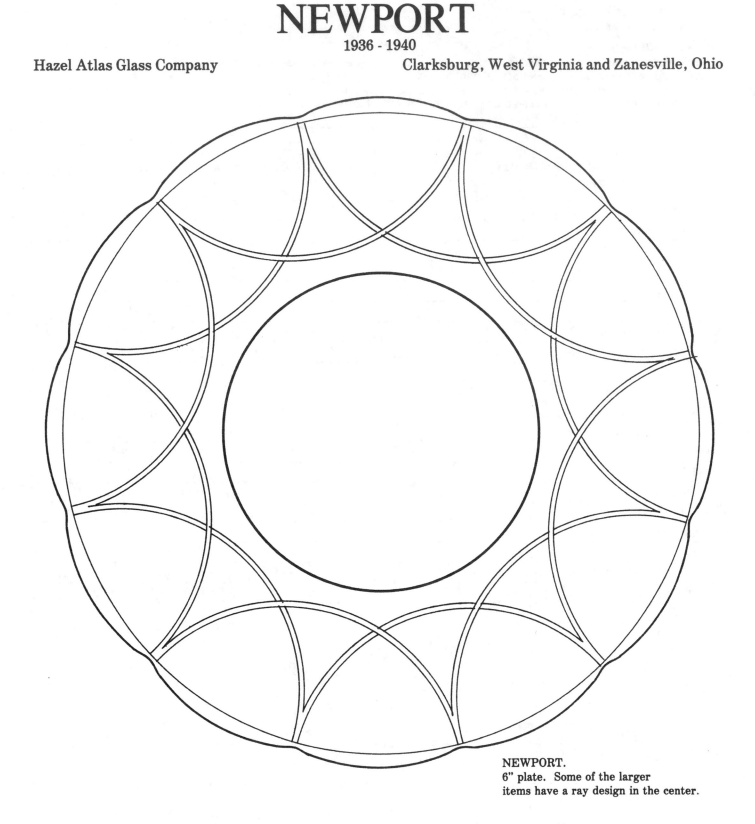

NEWPORT.
6" plate. Some of the larger
items have a ray design in the center.

**Colors found to date:**

- Amethyst ("Burgundy")   • Blue (Cobalt)   • Platonite (various colors)   • Pink

# NEWPORT

### Reproductions or reissues

None known to date.

### General pattern notes

Value for amethyst, cobalt blue, and a few pieces in pink are so nearly the same that the listing here lumps them together. The other colors would be valued at about one-half or a little more of the values listed.

Newport is sometimes called "Hairpin."

| ITEM & DESCRIPTION | DOLLAR VALUE RANGES BY COLOR | |
| --- | --- | --- |
| | Cobalt Blue or Amethyst | Platonite (White) |
| Bowl, 4-1/4" | 18-24 | 4-5 |
| Bowl, 4-3/4" (cream soup) | 20-22 | 8-10 |
| Bowl, 5-1/4" | 35-40 | 8-10 |
| Bowl, 8-1/4" | 42-46 | 10-12 |
| Cup | 12-14 | 4-5 |
| Creamer | 14-16 | 4-5 |
| Plate, 6" | 8-10 | 3-4 |
| Plate, 8-1/2" | 14-20 | 6-8 |
| Plate, 11-1/2" | 40-45 | 10-12 |
| Platter, 11-3/4" (oval) | 45-50 | 12-14 |
| Salt and pepper (shakers, pair) | 60-70 | 24-28 |
| Saucer | 4-5 | 1-2 |
| Sherbet | 16-18 | 4-5 |
| Sugar | 14-16 | 4-5 |
| Tumbler, 4-1/2" | 40-45 | 6-8 |

# NORMANDIE

1933 - 1940

Federal Glass Company                                   Columbus, Ohio

Colors found to date:

• Amber             • Crystal             • Pink

# NORMANDIE

**Reproductions or reissues**

None known to date.

**General pattern notes**

There are some who call this pattern "Bouquet and Lattice."

Some iridescent items are showing up and they tend to bring a bit higher price than the other pieces in isolated cases.

The pattern was first produced in pink and crystal, followed by an iridescent amber, then a true clear amber.

The salt and pepper shakers, pitchers, and covered sugars are the most sought-after items in this pattern.

| ITEM & DESCRIPTION | DOLLAR VALUE RANGES BY COLOR | | |
|---|---|---|---|
| | Amber | Iridescent | Pink |
| Bowl, 5" | 6-8 | 4-5 | 10-12 |
| Bowl, 6-1/2" | 20-24 | 8-10 | 30-35 |
| Bowl, 8-1/2" | 20-24 | 14-16 | 30-35 |
| Bowl, 10" (oval) | 20-24 | 16-18 | 40-45 |
| Creamer (footed) | 10-12 | 8-10 | 14-16 |
| Cup | 8-10 | 5-6 | 10-12 |
| Pitcher, 8" | 85-95 | — | 175-195 |
| Plate, 6" | 4-6 | 3-5 | 6-8 |
| Plate, 8" | 10-12 | 40-45 | 14-16 |
| Plate, 9-1/4" | 12-14 | 12-14 | 16-18 |
| Plate, 11" | 40-45 | 10-12 | 150-175 |
| Plate, 11" (grill) | 16-18 | 10-12 | 125-145 |
| Platter, 11-3/4" | 30-35 | 12-14 | 34-36 |
| Salt and pepper (shakers, pair) | 50-60 | — | 85-95 |
| Saucer | 3-4 | 3-4 | 4-6 |
| Sherbet | 6-8 | 4-6 | 8-10 |
| Sugar | 10-12 | — | — |
| Sugar cover | 95-110 | — | 200-250 |
| Tumbler, 4" | 35-45 | — | 95-110 |
| Tumbler, 4-1/4" | 30-35 | — | 75-85 |
| Tumbler, 5" | 45-50 | — | 120-130 |

# OLD CAFE
## 1936-1940

Hocking Glass Company

Lancaster, Ohio

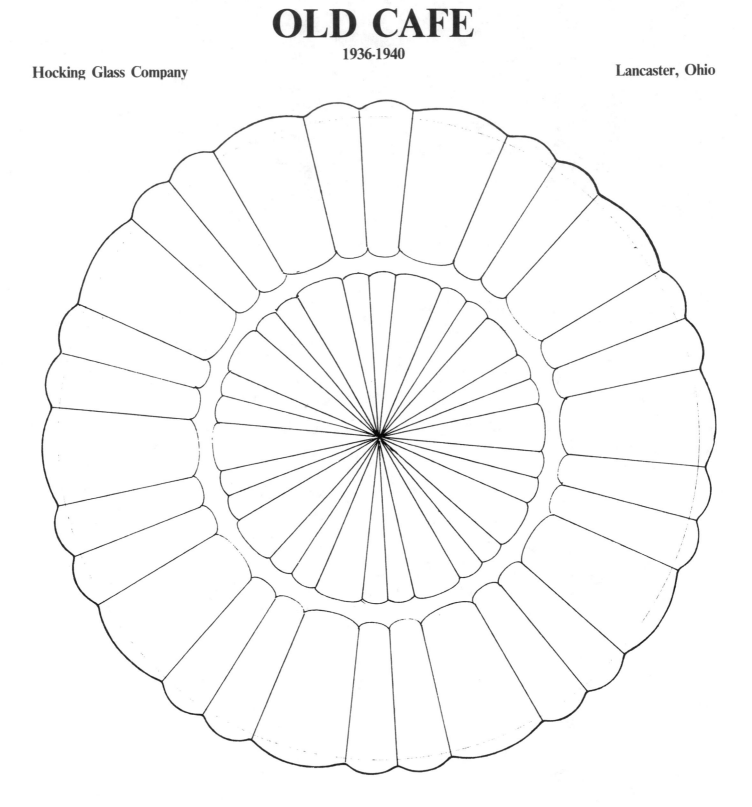

**Colors found to date:**

- Royal Ruby Red 1940
- Crystal 1936-1938
- Pink 1936-1938

# OLD CAFÉ

**Reproductions or reissues**

None known to date.

**General pattern notes**

In 1940, Hocking made a few assorted pieces in its Royal Ruby Red color. It is known that it sometimes mixed crystal and red in items such as cups and saucers and covered candy dishes. The pitchers are scarce in all colors.

| ITEM & DESCRIPTION | DOLLAR VALUE RANGES BY COLOR | | |
|---|---|---|---|
| | Crystal | Pink | Royal Ruby |
| Bowl, 3-3/4" | 2-3 | 4-6 | 8-10 |
| Bowl, 5", two handled | 2-3 | 4-6 | 10-12 |
| Bowl, 5-1/2" | 5-7 | 10-15 | 18-20 |
| Bowl, 9", two handled, closed | 9-10 | 18-20 | 24-26 |
| Candy, 8", covered | 9-10 | 18-20 | 16-18 |
| Cup | 3-6 | 6-12 | 10-12 |
| Lamp | 75-90 | 150-175 | 150-160 |
| Pickle or olive dish, 6", handled, oblong | 5-6 | 10-12 | — |
| Pitcher, 6", 36 oz. | 35-40 | 75-85 | — |
| Pitcher, 9", 80 oz. | 50-60 | 100-125 | — |
| Plate, 6" | 2-6 | 4-12 | — |
| Plate, 10" | 15-20 | 35-45 | — |
| Saucer | 1-5 | 2-10 | — |
| Sherbet, footed | 5-6 | 10-12 | 15-18 |
| Tumbler, 3" | 7-8 | 14-16 | — |
| Tumbler, 4" | 9-10 | 18-20 | — |
| Vase, 7-1/4" | 15-17 | 30-35 | 35-40 |

# OYSTER AND PEARLS

## 1938 - 1940

### Anchor-Hocking Glass Corporation

**Colors found to date:**

- Crystal
- Opaque White
- Pink
- Ruby Red

# OYSTERS AND PEARLS

**Reproductions or reissues**

None known to date.

**General pattern notes**

Only a small number of items are available in this pattern. They are all accessory or serving pieces.
The opaque white pieces are white on the outside and pink or green on the inside.

| ITEM & DESCRIPTION | DOLLAR VALUE RANGES BY COLOR | | | |
|---|---|---|---|---|
| | Crystal fired-on Green or Pink | Pink | Red | Opaque white with fired-on Green or Pink |
| Bowl, 5-1/4" | 5-6 | 10-12 | 20-24 | 6-8 |
| Bowl, 5-1/4" (heart shape) | 5-6 | 10-12 | 20-24 | 6-8 |
| Bowl, 6-1/2" (handled) | 14-15 | 28-30 | 28-30 | 14-16 |
| Bowl, 10-1/2" | 19-20 | 38-40 | 50-60 | 18-20 |
| Candleholder, 3-1/2" (pair) | 13-14 | 26-28 | 50-60 | 12-15 |
| Plate, 13-1/2" | 15-17 | 30-35 | 50-60 | — |
| Relish dish, 10-1/4" (two sections) | 15-17 | 30-35 | — | 10-12 |

# PARROT
### 1931 - 1932

Federal Glass Company                                    Columbus, Ohio

**Colors found to date:**

- Amber          - Blue*          - Crystal          - Green

*Only one piece known at present, but lends evidence that there might be more.

# PARROT

## Reproductions or reissues

None known to date.

## General pattern notes

Parrot is also sometimes known as "Sylvan." Sylvan was the name given the pattern by the company, but it is much better known and identified by the name "Parrot."

The pattern was in production for only a very short period of time.

Green is the color found most often, followed by amber. The other colors are in short supply.

| ITEM & DESCRIPTION | DOLLAR VALUE RANGES BY COLOR | |
| --- | --- | --- |
| | Amber | Green |
| Bowl, 5" | 22-24 | 30-35 |
| Bowl, 7" | 35-40 | 50-55 |
| Bowl, 8" | 75-85 | 95-100 |
| Bowl, 10" (oval) | 65-75 | 50-60 |
| Butter dish and cover | 1,100-1,200 | 400-450 |
| Creamer (footed) | 65-75 | 55-65 |
| Cup | 40-45 | 38-40 |
| Hot plate, 5" | 850-950 | 850-950 |
| Pitcher, 8-1/2" | — | 2,200-2,400 |
| Plate, 5-3/4" | 26-28 | 30-35 |
| Plate, 7-1/2" | — | 35-40 |
| Plate, 9" | 45-50 | 55-60 |
| Plate, 10-1/2" (grill, round) | — | 60-70 |
| Plate, 10-1/2" (grill, square) | 45-50 | — |
| Platter, 11-1/4" | 75-80 | 50-60 |
| Salt and pepper (shakers, pair) | — | 250-275 |
| Saucer | 12-14 | 12-14 |
| Sherbet (footed) | 24-26 | 28-30 |
| Sherbet, 4-1/4" | — | 1,200-1,300 |
| Sugar | 35-40 | 40-45 |
| Sugar cover | 450-500 | 175-200 |
| Tumbler, 4-1/4" | 110-125 | 150-175 |
| Tumbler, 5-1/2" | 145-155 | 175-195 |
| Tumbler, 5-3/4" (footed) | 110-125 | 125-145 |

# PATRICIAN

### 1933 - 1937

Federal Glass Company                                                                 Columbus, Ohio

**Colors found to date:**

• Amber          • Crystal          • Green          • Pink

# PATRICIAN

## Reproductions or reissues
None known to date.

## General pattern notes
The company named this pattern "Spoke," but it is more popularly known as "Patrician."

Amber is the more commonly collected color because there is more of it available. There are, however, shortages in some amber pieces due to its popularity.

Covered pieces, pitchers, and tumblers in any color are the most desirable; therefore, values are high, relative to the rest of the collection.

| ITEM & DESCRIPTION | DOLLAR VALUE RANGES BY COLOR | | |
| --- | --- | --- | --- |
| | Amber or Crystal | Green | Pink |
| Bowl, 4-3/4" (cream soup) | 16-18 | 22-24 | 20-22 |
| Bowl, 5" | 12-14 | 12-14 | 12-14 |
| Bowl, 6" | 24-26 | 28-30 | 24-26 |
| Bowl, 8-1/2" | 40-45 | 38-40 | 28-30 |
| Bowl, 10" (oval) | 28-30 | 38-40 | 30-35 |
| Butter dish and cover | 100-110 | 120-125 | 200-225 |
| Cookie jar and cover | 85-95 | 550-600 | — |
| Creamer (footed) | 10-12 | 10-12 | 10-12 |
| Cup | 8-10 | 12-14 | 10-12 |
| Pitcher, 8" | 120-125 | 125-145 | 125-130 |
| Pitcher, 8-1/4" | 100-120 | 165-175 | 140-150 |
| Plate, 6" | 8-10 | 10-12 | 10-12 |
| Plate, 7-1/2" | 14-16 | 14-16 | 18-20 |
| Plate, 9" | 12-14 | 14-16 | 12-14 |
| Plate, 10-1/2" | 8-10 | 40-45 | 30-35 |
| Plate, 10-1/2" (grill) | 14-16 | 18-20 | 18-20 |
| Platter, 11-1/2" (oval) | 25-30 | 30-35 | 30-35 |
| Salt and pepper (pair) | 50-60 | 65-75 | 85-95 |
| Saucer | 6-8 | 8-10 | 8-10 |
| Sherbet | 10-12 | 12-14 | 12-14 |
| Sugar | 10-12 | 10-12 | 10-12 |
| Sugar cover | 50-60 | 65-70 | 60-65 |
| Tumbler, 4" | 28-30 | 30-35 | 30-35 |
| Tumbler, 4-1/2" | 28-30 | 26-28 | 24-26 |
| Tumbler, 5-1/2" | 40-45 | 40-45 | 35-40 |
| Tumbler, 5-1/4" (footed) | 60-70 | 65-70 | — |

# PEACOCK AND ROSE (No. 300)

### 1928 - 1930's

Paden City Glass Manufacturing Company

Paden City, West Virginia

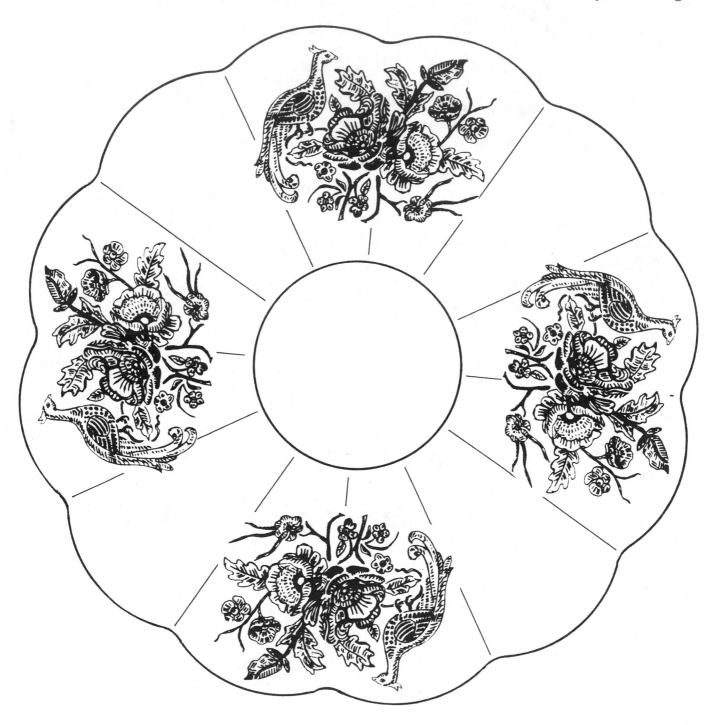

**Colors found to date:**

- Blue (Cobalt)
- Green
- Pink

# PEACOCK AND ROSES (No. 300)

**Reproductions or reissues**
    None known to date.

**General pattern notes**
    Paden City's number-300 line consists of many items. The blanks were utilized widely by the company for etching all sorts of designs. The Peacock and Rose design is very hard to find, with cups being the rarest.

| ITEM & DESCRIPTION | DOLLAR VALUE RANGES BY COLOR |
| --- | --- |
| | Green or Pink |
| Bowl, 8-1/2" | 120-135 |
| Bowl, 8-1/2" (oval, footed) | 160-170 |
| Bowl, 8-3/4" (footed) | 175-195 |
| Bowl, 9-1/4" (center handle) | 145-160 |
| Bowl, 10-1/2" | 165-175 |
| Bowl, 10-1/2" (footed) | 185-195 |
| Bowl, 10-1/2" (center handle) | 125-145 |
| Bowl, 11" (console, rolled edges) | 160-170 |
| Bowl, 14" (rolled edges) | 225-245 |
| Cake plate | 140-150 |
| Candlesticks (pair) | 175-195 |
| Candy dish and cover (footed) | 225-240 |
| Compote, 6-1/4" | 100-125 |
| Creamer, 4-1/2" (footed) | 60-70 |
| Cup | 75-85 |
| Ice bucket, 5-3/4" | 165-195 |
| Mayonnaise set (three pieces) | 100-125 |
| Plate, 8" | 40-50 |
| Plate, 10-1/2" | 100-110 |
| Relish | 85-95 |
| Saucer | 15-18 |
| Sugar, 4-1/4" | 60-70 |
| Vase, 10" | 195-225 |

# PEANUT BUTTER
## 1950 s

**Manufacturer Unknown**

Colors found to date:

• Crystal, tumblers and sherbets in milk glass

# PEANUT BUTTER

**Reproductions or reissues**

None known to date.

**General pattern notes**

Very little is known about this pattern other than the fact that the water glass was the container in which Big Top Peanut Butter was sold in the early- to mid-1950s. Only five other pieces have turned up so far. It has been reported that the water glass and sherbet have shown up in milk glass. This is as yet unsubstantiated. Crystal is the color you will find this pattern in.

| ITEM & DESCRIPTION | DOLLAR VALUE RANGE BY COLOR |
| --- | --- |
| | Crystal |
| Plate, 8" | 3-4 |
| Cup | 1-2 |
| Saucer | 1-2 |
| Sherbet (footed) | 3-4 |
| Juice Glass, 5-1/4" | 4-5 |
| Water Glass, 5-3/4" | 2-4 |

# PETALWARE
## 1930 - 1940

Macbeth-Evans Glass Company                                    Charleroi, Pennsylvania

Colors found to date:

- Cobalt Blue
- Monax
- Cremax
- Pink
- Crystal
- Various fired on colors

# PETALWARE

## Reproductions or reissues

None known to date.

## General pattern notes

In 1930, Macbeth-Evans released Petalware in pink and crystal. In the following years, it added many variations of the cremax and monax by painting different colorful designs on them.

Only four pieces are known to exist presently in the cobalt blue. These are the 8-3/4-inch bowl, the footed creamer, footed sherbet, and footed sugar bowl. All are worth in excess of $30. There is a fifth piece in cobalt, the metal mustard cover, but it is fairly common and valued at only about $7-$8.

The values listed below are for all colors and designs.

| ITEM & DESCRIPTION | DOLLAR VALUE RANGES BY COLOR |
| --- | --- |
| | All colors |
| Bowl, 4-1/2" (cream soup) | 5-15 |
| Bowl, 5-3/4" | 5-15 |
| Bowl, 7" | 60-70 |
| Bowl, 8-3/4" | 8-30 |
| Cup | 5-10 |
| Creamer | 5-15 |
| Lamp shade (two sizes) | 15-25 |
| Mustard with metal cover | 8-10 |
| Pitcher | 24-28 |
| Plate, 6" | 4-8 |
| Plate, 8" | 4-10 |
| Plate, 9" | 5-20 |
| Plate, 11" | 10-20 |
| Plate, 12" | 10-20 |
| Platter, 13" (oval) | 10-30 |
| Saucer | 1-5 |
| Sherbet, 4" (footed) | 18-20 |
| Sherbet, 4-1/2" (footed) | 3-15 |
| Sugar (footed) | 5-15 |
| Tidbit servers | 14-25 |
| Tumblers | 8-12 |

# PINEAPPLE AND FLORAL (No. 618)
## 1932 - 1937

Indiana Glass Company

Dunkirk, Indiana

Colors found to date:

- Amber
- Crystal
- Green
- Red (fired-on color)
- White

# PINEAPPLE AND FLORAL (No. 618)

**Reproductions or reissues**

There were some pieces reissued in the 1970s in an avocado green and milk white.

**General pattern notes**

The amber and fired-on red color are the more valuable pieces in this pattern. Although there are no extraordinarily high value items in the pattern, the tumblers and most of the bowls are becoming hard to find.

| ITEMS & DESCRIPTION | DOLLAR VALUE RANGES BY COLOR | |
| --- | --- | --- |
| | Amber or Red | Crystal |
| Ashtray | — | 6-8 |
| Bowl, 4-3/4" | 6-8 | 4-6 |
| Bowl, 6" | 8-10 | 6-8 |
| Bowl, 7" | 12-14 | 6-8 |
| Bowl (cream soup) | 12-14 | 8-10 |
| Bowl, 10" (oval) | 10-12 | 8-10 |
| Compote (diamond shape) | 8-10 | 4-6 |
| Creamer (diamond shape) | 4-5 | 2-3 |
| Cup | 4-5 | 4-5 |
| Plate, 6" | 4-5 | 4-5 |
| Plate, 8-3/8" | 8-10 | 6-8 |
| Plate, 9-1/2" | 14-16 | 14-16 |
| Plate, 11-1/2" | 12-14 | 14-16 |
| Platter, 11" (closed handles) | 14-16 | 10-12 |
| Platter, 11-1/2" (relish, sectioned) | 10-12 | 8-10 |
| Saucer | 1-2 | 1-2 |
| Sherbet (footed) | 6-8 | 4-6 |
| Sugar (diamond shape) | 4-5 | 2-3 |
| Tumbler, 4-1/4" | 16-18 | 12-14 |
| Tumbler, 4-1/2" | 18-20 | 14-16 |
| Vase (cone shape, with metal holder) | — | 12-14 |

# PRETZEL

1930 s-1970 s

Indiana Glass Company

Dunkirk, Indiana

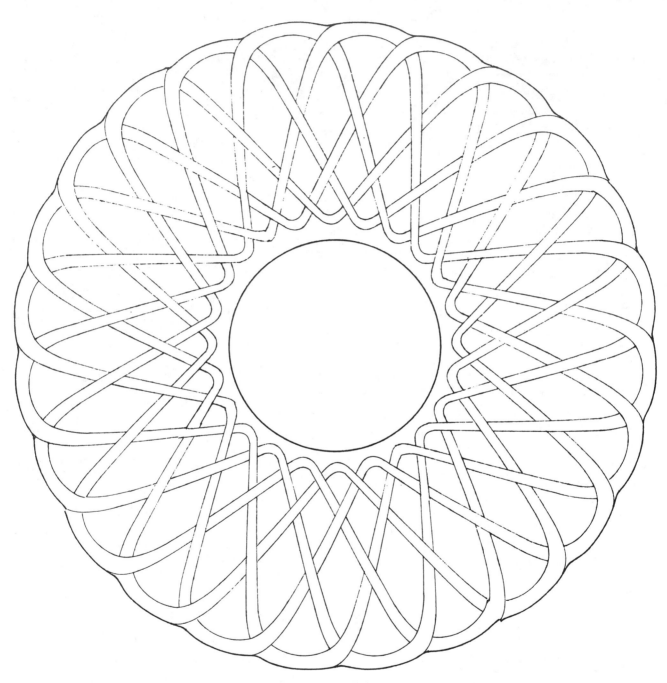

# PRETZEL

**Reproductions or reissues**

The two-handled pickle dish, leaf-shaped olive dish, and the celery dish have all been made in quantity into the 1970s.

**General pattern notes**

The company catalogs identified this pattern only as No. 622, but collectors have dubbed it "Pretzel" for obvious reasons. It is an inexpensive pattern to collect, but has a limited number of pieces in the line. A pitcher and three sizes of tumblers may be found. They are listed in catalogs, but it is not known that any have ever turned up. The company may never have produced them.

| ITEM & DESCRIPTION | DOLLAR VALUE RANGE BY COLOR |
|---|---|
| | Crystal |
| Bowl, 7-1/2" | 8-10 |
| Bowl, 9-3/8" | 14-16 |
| Celery dish, 10-1/4" | 4-5 |
| Creamer | 5-6 |
| Sugar | 5-6 |
| Cup | 3-4 |
| Saucer | 1-2 |
| Olive dish (leaf shaped), 7" | 5-6 |
| Pickle dish (two-handled), 8-1/2" | 6-7 |
| Pickle dish (tab handled) | 3-4 |
| Plate, 6" | 4-5 |
| Plate, 8-3/8" | 6-8 |
| Plate, 9-3/8" | 8-10 |
| Plate, 11-1/2" | 10-12 |
| Sherbet | 5-6 |

# PRINCESS

## 1931 - 1935

Hocking Glass Company

(now Anchor-Hocking Glass Corporation)

**Colors found to date:**

- Amber (Topaz or Dark Yellow)
- Pink
- *Blue
- Yellow
- Green

*Suspected to be a reproduction from Mexico. This is not substantiated.

# PRINCESS

**Reproductions or reissues**

Suspected. See footnote on previous page.

**General pattern notes**

First to be produced in 1931 was the green and then came the dark yellow color (amber to topaz), but the darker yellow was soon discontinued.

Rarest of the items in this pattern are the pitchers (footed), a six-inch yellow pitcher, and yellow covered butter dishes.

Hocking also used a frosted finish on some of its Princess items.

There is no true saucer for cups in this pattern. They are the same as the 5-1/2-inch sherbet plates.

| ITEM & DESCRIPTION | DOLLAR VALUE RANGES BY COLOR | | |
|---|---|---|---|
| | Green | Pink | Yellow |
| Ashtray | 65-75 | 85-95 | 110-120 |
| Bowl, 4-1/2" | 24-26 | 26-28 | 45-50 |
| Bowl, 5" | 35-40 | 38-40 | 32-35 |
| Bowl, 9" (octagonal) | 35-40 | 35-40 | 125-145 |
| Bowl, 9-1/2" (hat shape) | 60-70 | 55-60 | 145-160 |
| Bowl, 10" (oval) | 28-30 | 24-26 | 50-60 |
| Butter dish and cover | 100-120 | 110-125 | 600-700 |
| Cake stand, 10" | 30-35 | 35-40 | — |
| Candy dish and cover | 65-75 | 70-80 | — |
| Coaster | 65-75 | 75-85 | 110-120 |
| Cookie jar and cover | 60-70 | 75-85 | — |
| Creamer (oval) | 14-16 | 12-14 | 18-20 |
| Cup | 12-14 | 10-12 | 8-10 |
| Pitcher, 6" | 55-60 | 65-75 | 650-700 |
| Pitcher, 7-3/8" (footed) | 600-700 | 400-450 | — |
| Pitcher, 8" | 55-60 | 55-60 | 110-125 |
| Plate, 5-1/2" (used as saucer) | 8-10 | 8-10 | 6-8 |
| Plate, 8" | 12-14 | 14-16 | 14-16 |
| Plate, 9-1/2" | 28-30 | 16-28 | 24-26 |
| Plate, 9-1/2" (grill) | 14-16 | 14-16 | 8-10 |
| Plate, 11-1/2" (grill, closed handle) | 10-12 | 10-12 | 8-10 |
| Plate, 11-1/2" (handled) | 18-20 | 18-20 | 150-160 |
| Platter, 12" (closed handles) | 26-28 | 26-28 | 50-60 |
| Relish, 7-1/2" (sectioned) | 24-26 | 28-30 | 85-95 |
| Relish, 7-1/2" (no sections) | 200-225 | 175-195 | 225-250 |
| Salt and pepper, 4-1/2" (pair) | 55-60 | 50-55 | 75-85 |
| Spice shakers, 5-1/2" (pair) | 35-40 | — | — |
| Sherbet (footed) | 20-24 | 20-24 | 25-30 |
| Sugar and cover | 35-40 | 30-35 | 35-40 |
| Tumbler, 3" | 30-35 | 30-35 | 30-35 |
| Tumbler, 4" | 28-30 | 28-30 | 24-26 |
| Tumbler, 5-1/4" | 45-50 | 30-35 | — |
| Tumbler, 4-3/4" (footed) | 60-65 | 55-60 | — |
| Tumbler, 5-1/4" (footed) | 28-30 | 28-30 | 24-28 |
| Tumbler, 6-1/2" (footed) | 110-125 | 85-95 | 150-160 |
| Vase, 8" | 40-45 | 45-50 | — |

# PYRAMID (No. 610)
### c. 1930

Indiana Glass Company

Dunkirk, Indiana

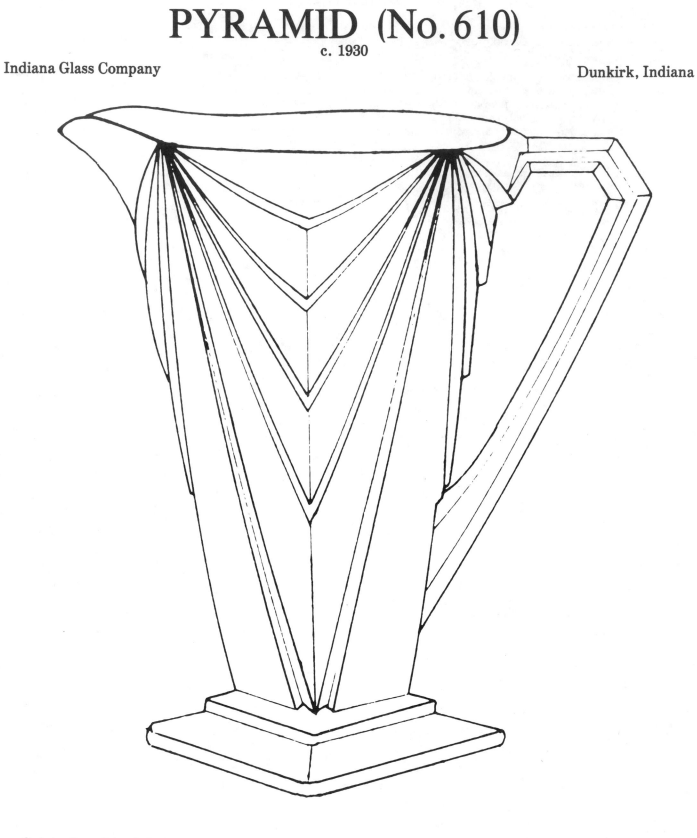

**Colors found to date:**

- Black
- Pink
- Crystal
- White (Opaque)
- Green
- Yellow

# PYRAMID (No. 610)

## Reproductions or reissues

Pyramid has been reissued twice. In the 1950s, it was reissued in opaque white and topaz. In 1974, the company began producing the pattern in black for distribution through Tiara Home Products and it was distributed exclusively through Tiara at home-party sales.

## General pattern notes

This pattern was apparently produced only in accessory tableware, for there are no cups, dinner plates, etc.; primarily serving pieces. There seems to be a dire shortage of any items in crystal, so be on the lookout for them. They should bring a premium price.

| ITEM & DESCRIPTION | DOLLAR VALUE RANGES BY COLOR | | |
|---|---|---|---|
| | Pink | Green | Yellow |
| Bowl, 4-3/4" | 28-30 | 28-30 | 38-40 |
| Bowl, 8-1/2" | 40-45 | 40-45 | 65-70 |
| Bowl, 9-1/2" (oval) | 40-45 | 40-45 | 60-65 |
| Bowl, 9-1/2" | 38-40 | 38-40 | 55-60 |
| Creamer | 30-35 | 30-35 | 40-45 |
| Ice tub | 110-125 | 110-125 | 175-195 |
| Ice tub and cover | — | — | 750-800 |
| Pitcher | 300-325 | 325-350 | 495-550 |
| Relish tray (handled, four sections) | 45-50 | 50-55 | 65-75 |
| Sugar | 38-40 | 38-40 | 40-45 |
| Tray for creamer and sugar | 28-30 | 30-35 | 50-55 |
| Tumbler, 8 oz. (footed) | 45-50 | 55-60 | 85-95 |
| Tumbler, 11 oz. (footed) | 65-75 | 75-80 | 110-120 |

# QUEEN MARY
### 1936 - 1940 s

Hocking Glass Company

(now Anchor-Hocking Glass Corporation)

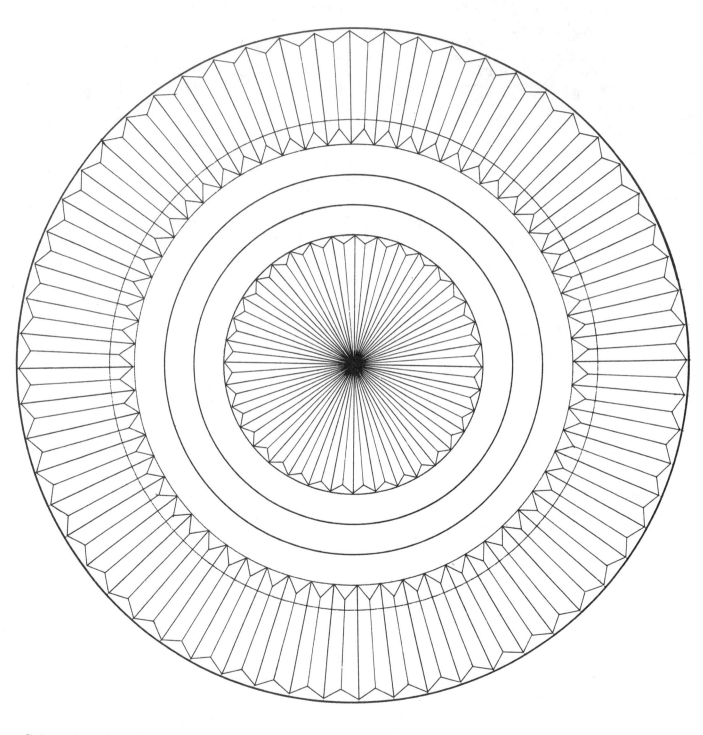

Colors found to date:

- Crystal
- *Green
- Pink
- Red (Ruby)

*Ash tray only. Made in the 1950 s.

# QUEEN MARY

**Reproductions or reissues**

None known to date.

**General pattern notes**

Sometimes called "Vertical Ribbed," Queen Mary was first produced in pink, then came crystal. The ruby red was the latest, being released in the 1940s.

There are two distinct types of cups to be found.

The butter dish with cover, candy dish with cover, 9-3/4-inch plate, and salt and pepper shakers, when found in pink, are worth anywhere from two to five times the values listed below.

| ITEM & DESCRIPTION | DOLLAR VALUE RANGES BY COLOR | |
|---|---|---|
| | Crystal | Pink |
| Ashtray, 2" x 3-3/4" (oval) | 1-3 | 3-6 |
| Bowl, 4" (one handle or no handle) | 2-3 | 5-7 |
| Bowl, 5" | 2-3 | 5-7 |
| Bowl, 5-1/2" (two-handled) | 4-9 | 8-18 |
| Bowl, 6" | 4-10 | 8-20 |
| Bowl, 7" | 4-6 | 8-12 |
| Bowl, 8-3/4" | 7-10 | 14-20 |
| Butter dish and cover | 10-60 | 20-120 |
| Candy dish and cover | 10-30 | 20-60 |
| Candlesticks, 4-1/2" (pair) | 10-15 | 20-30 |
| Candlesticks (red) | 30-35 | 65-75 |
| Celery dish, 5" x 10" | 6-17 | 12-35 |
| Cigarette box (oval) | 5-9 | 10-18 |
| Coaster, 3-1/2" | 2-5 | 5-10 |
| Coaster, 4-1/4" (square) | 2-6 | 5-12 |
| Compote, 5-3/4" | 7-12 | 15-25 |
| Creamer (oval) | 4-17 | 8-15 |
| Cup (two styles) | 2-6 | 5-12 |
| Plate, 6" | 2-4 | 4-8 |
| Plate, 6-5/8" | 2-4 | 4-8 |
| Plate, 8-1/2" | 2-3 | 5-6 |
| Plate, 9-3/4" | 10-30 | 20-60 |
| Plate, 12" | 7-14 | 15-28 |
| Plate, 14" | 6-10 | 12-20 |
| *Punch bowl set (six cups, bowl, metal rim for bowl, and ladle) | 1,200-1,500 | 2,500-3,000 |
| Relish tray, 12" (three sections) | 5-17 | 10-35 |
| Relish tray, 14" (four sections) | 6-17 | 12-35 |
| Salt and pepper (shakers, pair) | 9-12 | 18-24 |
| Saucer | 1-3 | 2-5 |
| Sherbet (footed) | 3-5 | 6-10 |
| Sugar (oval) | 4-7 | 8-15 |
| Tumbler, 3-1/2" | 3-8 | 6-16 |
| Tumbler, 4" | 4-9 | 8-18 |
| Tumbler, 5" (footed) | 15-35 | 30-75 |
| *It is not likely that the metal lid and ladle will be found, but, if so, what a lucky find! | | |

# RADIANCE

1935-1940

New Martinsville Glass Company

**Colors Found To Date**
- Amber
- Cobalt
- Crystal
- Ice Blue
- Red

# RADIANCE

**Reproductions or reissues**

None known to date.

**General pattern notes**

You will note in the value-range listing below that the crystal items are lower than the others. If they are found with silver or gold rims or decorations, they will command the same prices in the others. Cobalt is the rarest color.

| ITEM & DESCRIPTION | DOLLAR VALUE RANGES BY COLOR | | |
|---|---|---|---|
| | Crystal | Red | Amber-Ice Blue |
| Bowl (two-handled), 5" | 4-5 | 18-20 | 8-10 |
| Bowl, 6" | 4-5 | 18-20 | 8-10 |
| Bowl (footed), 6" | 5-6 | 20-24 | 10-12 |
| Bowl (covered), 6" | 15-20 | 70-80 | 35-40 |
| Bowl (two-section relish), 7" | 12-15 | 50-60 | 28-30 |
| Bowl (three-section relish) | 12-15 | 50-60 | 28-30 |
| Bowl, 7" | 6-7 | 24-28 | 12-14 |
| Bowl (ruffled edge), 10" | 12-15 | 48-50 | 24-26 |
| Bowl (ruffled edge), 12" | 12-15 | 50-60 | 28-30 |
| Bowl (flared edge), 10" | 12-15 | 50-60 | 28-30 |
| Bowl (flared edge), 12" | 12-15 | 50-60 | 28-30 |
| Butter dish | 40-50 | 180-200 | 80-100 |
| Candleholder, 8" | 25-30 | 100-110 | 50-60 |
| Candle holder (two branch) | 30-35 | 125-135 | 65-70 |
| Celery dish, 10" | 8-10 | 36-40 | 18-20 |
| Cheese and cracker set, 11" | 20-25 | 80-100 | 45-60 |
| Compote, 5" | 10-12 | 35-45 | 20-22 |
| Compote, 6" | 10-12 | 45-50 | 22-24 |
| Condiment set (four pieces) | 60-70 | 280-295 | 140-160 |
| Creamer | 8-10 | 35-40 | 18-20 |
| Sugar | 8-10 | 35-40 | 18-20 |
| Cruet (individual size) | 18-20 | 65-95 | 36-40 |
| Cup | 6-8 | 24-26 | 12-14 |
| Saucer | 2-3 | 8-10 | 4-6 |
| Decanter and stopper | 50-60 | 195-225 | 100-120 |
| Lamp, 12" | 30-35 | 125-145 | 65-75 |
| Mayonnaise set (three pieces) | 30-35 | 120-140 | 60-70 |
| Pitcher, 64 oz. (cobalt: 318-338) | 90-100 | 350-400 | 180-200 |
| Plate, 8" | 5-6 | 20-24 | 10-12 |
| Plate, 14" (punch bowl base) | 22-25 | 85-95 | 45-50 |
| Punch bowl | 50-60 | 195-225 | 100-125 |
| Punch bowl ladle | 50-60 | 195-225 | 100-125 |
| Punch cup | 4-5 | 16-18 | 8-10 |
| Salt and pepper | 30-35 | 120-140 | 60-70 |
| Tray (oval) | 10-12 | 40-45 | 20-24 |
| Tumbler, 9 oz. (cobalt: 36-41) | 10-12 | 40-45 | 20-24 |
| Vase, 10" | 25-30 | 95-125 | 50-60 |
| Vase, 12" | 45-50 | 195-225 | 95-100 |

# RAINDROPS
## 1927-1933
## See "Thumbprint"

Manufactured by Federal Glass Company, Columbus, Ohio.

### Colors found to date
Crystal and green.

### Reproductions or reissues
None known to exist.

### General pattern notes
"Raindrops" was first produced in 1927 in green tumblers only. Then came the rest of the line by 1929.

This pattern is frequently confused with another similar pattern by Federal. "Thumbprint" further confused here because there was no handy example piece of "Raindrops" to do a pattern drawing. If you will refer to the drawing of "Thumbprint" on Page 209, it will become clear what the major difference is. In that drawing, notice that the impressions are more or less pear-shaped. It is not clear in the drawing, but the pear-shaped impressions of Thumbprint are actually depressions in the glass. In Raindrops' pieces, the designs are round and are bumps, not depressions. Once you have handled both, you won't have any more trouble identifying them.

Covered sugars are the rarest of this pattern, along with a pair of salt and peppers. For some unknown reason, there is a shortage of pepper shakers.

Crystal pieces are seldom seen.

| ITEM & DESCRIPTION | DOLLAR VALUE RANGES BY COLOR | |
| --- | --- | --- |
| | Crystal | Green |
| Bowl, 4-1/2" | 2-3 | 5-6 |
| Bowl, 6" | 4-5 | 8-10 |
| Cup | 3-4 | 6-8 |
| Creamer | 3-4 | 6-8 |
| Plate, 6" | 1-2 | 3-4 |
| Plate, 8" | 2-3 | 5-6 |
| Salt and pepper (shakers, pair) | 125-135 | 250-275 |
| Saucer | .50-1 | 1-2 |
| Sherbet | 3-4 | 6-8 |
| Sugar | 3-4 | 6-8 |
| Sugar cover | 15-20 | 35-40 |
| Tumbler, 3" | 3-4 | 6-8 |
| Whiskey jigger, 1-7/8" | 4-5 | 8-10 |

# RIBBON

**1930 - 1931**

Hazel Atlas Glass Company                    Clarksburg, West Virginia and Zanesville, Ohio

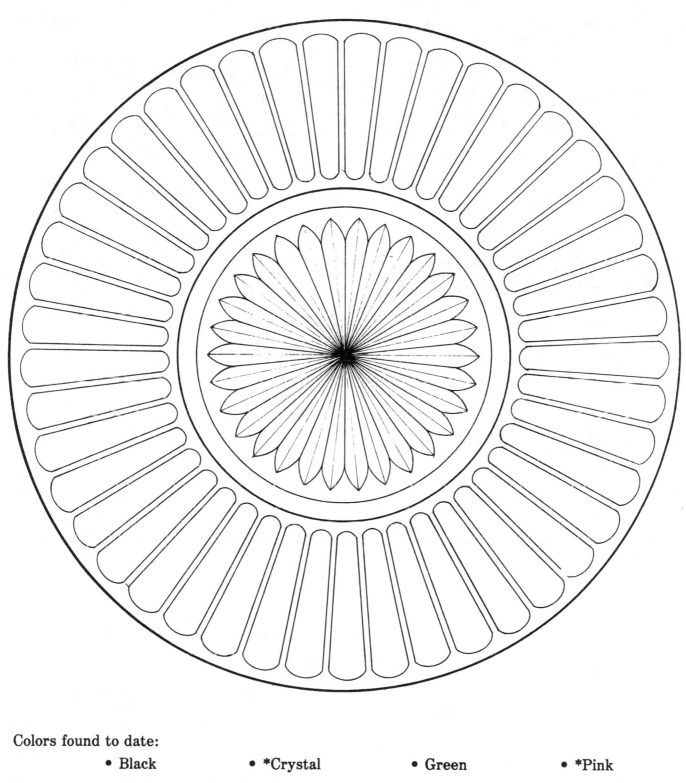

**Colors found to date:**

- Black          - *Crystal          - Green          - *Pink

*Few examples have been found so far.

# RIBBON

**Reproductions or reissues**

None known to date.

**General pattern notes**

The preponderance of color in this pattern is green. There are some black pieces, but they are not highly sought but by a few collectors.

A very short-lived pattern, Ribbon may become quite popular, owing to its fairly low prices. Remember what demand does to supply and prices.

As is the case so much of the time, it's hard to find the covers for several pieces; therefore, the covered candy dish in Ribbon commands the highest price in the pattern.

| ITEM & DESCRIPTION | DOLLAR VALUE RANGES BY COLOR | |
| --- | --- | --- |
| | Black | Green |
| Bowl, 4" | — | 25-30 |
| Bowl, 8" | 35-40 | 35-40 |
| Candy dish and cover | — | 35-40 |
| Creamer (footed) | — | 14-16 |
| Cup | — | 4-6 |
| Plate, 6-1/4" | — | 4-5 |
| Plate, 8" | 12-14 | 4-6 |
| Salt and pepper (shakers, pair) | 45-50 | 40-45 |
| Saucer | — | 2-3 |
| Sherbet (footed) | — | 5-6 |
| Sugar (footed) | — | 14-16 |
| Tumbler, 5-1/2" | — | 30-35 |

# ROSE CAMEO
## c. 1930

*Belmont Tumbler Company

Bellaire, Ohio

ROSE CAMEO. Border design detail. Turn to CAMEO by Hocking and note the very close similarity of the design so that you may learn how to keep from confusing them. The major difference is that ROSE CAMEO here has a rose within the cameo and CAMEO has a dancing girl in the cameo.

Colors found to date:

- Green only

# ROSE CAMEO

### Reproductions or reissues

None known to date.

### General pattern notes

Little is known about this pattern or its manufacturer at present. There is a patent of the design dated Dec. 1, 1931, and granted to a Howard A. Lay.

Rose Cameo is sometimes confused with Hocking's "Cameo," but all the collector has to do is note that there is no ballerina in the "Rose Cameo" design, to prevent the confusion.

So far, no cups and saucers have been found.

|  | DOLLAR VALUE RANGES BY COLOR |
| --- | --- |
| ITEM & DESCRIPTION | Green |
| Bowl, 4-1/2" | 12-15 |
| Bowl, 5" | 18-20 |
| Bowl, 6" | 25-30 |
| Plate, 7" | 14-16 |
| Sherbet | 14-16 |
| Tumbler, 5" (footed) | 24-26 |

# ROSEMARY
### 1935 - 1937

**Federal Glass Company**                    **Columbus, Ohio**

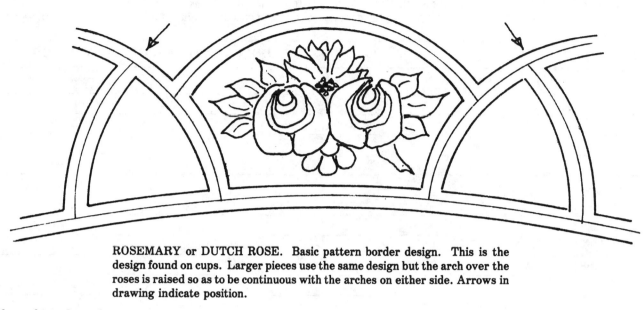

ROSEMARY or DUTCH ROSE. Basic pattern border design. This is the design found on cups. Larger pieces use the same design but the arch over the roses is raised so as to be continuous with the arches on either side. Arrows in drawing indicate position.

**Colors found to date:**

- Amber
- Crystal
- Green
- Pink

# ROSEMARY

**Reproductions or reissues**

None known to date.

**General pattern notes**

This is the final design that Federal settled upon after the "Mayfair" pattern was discontinued due to patent problems and the molds redesigned (see Page 124).

Amber is the color most easily found, but the most popular colors are the green and pink.

Rosemary is a simple attractive pattern, almost formal. It makes a very nice collection that is fairly inexpensive to put together.

| ITEM & DESCRIPTION | DOLLAR VALUE RANGES BY COLOR | |
| --- | --- | --- |
| | Amber | Green or Pink |
| Bowl, 5" | 6-8 | 12-15 |
| Bowl, 5" (cream soup) | 14-16 | 25-30 |
| Bowl, 6" | 30-35 | 40-45 |
| Bowl, 10" (oval) | 16-18 | 30-40 |
| Creamer (footed) | 8-10 | 12-18 |
| Cup | 5-6 | 8-10 |
| Plate, 6-3/4" | 5-6 | 8-10 |
| Plate, 9-1/2" | 8-10 | 16-20 |
| Plate, 9-1/2" (grill) | 8-10 | 16-20 |
| Platter, 12" (oval) | 18-20 | 24-30 |
| Saucer | 4-5 | 4-5 |
| Sugar (footed, no handle) | 8-10 | 12-18 |
| Tumbler, 4-1/4" | 30-32 | 35-45 |

# ROULETTE

**1936 - 1937**

Hocking Glass Company

(now Anchor-Hocking Glass Corporation)

Colors found to date:

- Crystal
- Green
- Pink

# ROULETTE

**Reproductions or reissues**

None known to date.

**General pattern notes**

Another simple, plain design that comes off almost elegant.

It was made in crystal throughout production, with some pink and green added. Prices for all of the colors are very close. Crystal may bring slightly more in some areas.

| ITEM & DESCRIPTION | DOLLAR VALUE RANGES BY COLOR |
|---|---|
| | All colors |
| Bowl, 9" | 10-24 |
| Cup | 4-8 |
| Pitcher, 8" | 30-50 |
| Plate, 6" | 4-6 |
| Plate, 8-1/2" | 4-8 |
| Plate, 12" | 8-18 |
| Saucer | 2-5 |
| Sherbet | 3-6 |
| Tumbler, 3-1/4", 5 oz. | 8-35 |
| Tumbler, 3-1/4" (old fashion) | 20-40 |
| Tumbler, 4-1/8" | 10-30 |
| Tumbler, 5-1/8" | 10-30 |
| Tumbler, 5-1/2" (footed) | 10-30 |
| Whiskey jiggers | 10-16 |

# ROUND ROBIN

## C. 1930
### Manufacturer unknown

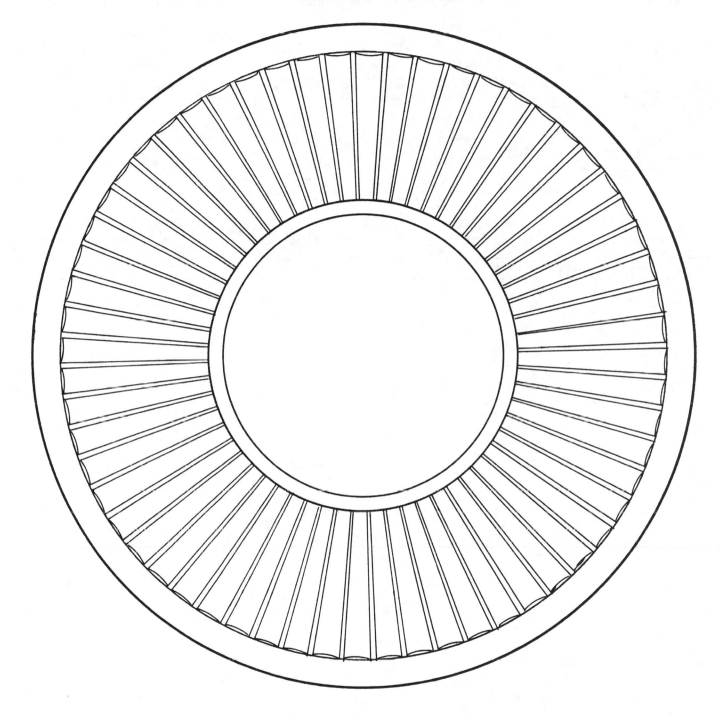

**Colors found to date:**

- Green
- Iridescent Amber

# ROUND ROBIN

**Reproductions or reissues**

None known to exist.

**General pattern notes**

The Domino tray in the value listing was apparently made to hold the creamer and surround it with cubes of sugar as made by Domino. Little is known about the origin of this pattern. Values for both colors are much the same, therefore, they are lumped together as one.

| ITEM & DESCRIPTION | DOLLAR VALUE RANGES BY COLOR |
| --- | --- |
| | All colors |
| Bowl, 4" | 4-10 |
| Cup (footed) | 5-7 |
| Creamer (footed) | 4-10 |
| Domino Tray (round) | 50-75 |
| Plate, 6" | 3-8 |
| Plate, 8" | 5-10 |
| Plate, 12" | 5-12 |
| Saucer | 2-3 |
| Sherbet | 4-10 |
| Sugar (footed) | 4-10 |

# ROXANA

c. 1930

*Hazel Atlas Glass Company                    Clarksburg, West Virginia and Zanesville, Ohio

Colors found to date:     • Yellow

*Strongly suspected to be the manufacturer of this pattern.

# ROXANA

**Reproductions or reissues**

None known to date.

**General pattern notes**

So far, only about six types of pieces have surfaced in this pattern. Little else is known.

| ITEM & DESCRIPTION | DOLLAR VALUE RANGES BY COLOR |
|---|---|
| | Yellow |
| Bowl, 4" | 18-20 |
| Bowl, 5" | 12-15 |
| Bowl, 6" | 18-20 |
| Plate, 6" | 10-12 |
| Sherbet (footed) | 10-12 |
| Tumbler, 4" | 20-22 |

# ROYAL LACE
### 1934 - 1941

Hazel Atlas Glass Company                    Clarksburg, West Virginia and Zanesville, Ohio

**Colors found to date:**

- Amethyst (Burgundy)
- Crystal
- Green
- Blue (Dark)
- Pink

# ROYAL LACE

**Reproductions or reissues**
   None known to date.

**General pattern notes**
   Pitchers are difficult to find. There were several design changes of pitchers over the years, as well as the console bowls and candle holders. As usual, the covers of many items were broken or lost, making them more scarce and costly than their corresponding bowls.
   The amethyst pieces are quite rare and command premium prices over the other colors.
   Popularity of the other colors waxes and wanes frequently. This is a highly popular pattern with collectors, and the color preference changes with the whims of the collectors.

| ITEM & DESCRIPTION | DOLLAR VALUE RANGES BY COLOR | | | |
|---|---|---|---|---|
| | **Blue** | **Crystal** | **Green** | **Pink** |
| Bowl, 4-3/4" | 45-50 | 12-15 | 35-40 | 28-30 |
| Bowl, 5" | 60-85 | 20-28 | 40-50 | 35-45 |
| Bowl, 10" (round) | 65-75 | 20-24 | 30-40 | 35-45 |
| Bowl, 10" (straight edge, three legs) | 95-100 | 30-40 | 65-75 | 55-65 |
| Bowl, 10" (rolled edge, three legs) | 600-700 | 225-250 | 125-150 | 100-125 |
| Bowl, 10" (ruffled edge, three legs) | 750-850 | 60-70 | 125-150 | 100-125 |
| Bowl, 11" (oval) | 75-85 | 40-45 | 50-60 | 45-55 |
| Butter dish and cover | 650-750 | 75-100 | 300-350 | 200-225 |
| Candlesticks | 165-175 | 65-75 | 85-95 | 65-75 |
| Candlesticks (rolled edge) | 450-500 | 85-95 | 150-175 | 135-145 |
| Candlesticks (ruffled edge) | 500-550 | 75-85 | 150-175 | 135-145 |
| Cookie jar and cover | 450-500 | 35-45 | 100-125 | 65-75 |
| Cream (footed) | 60-65 | 12-15 | 30-35 | 22-24 |
| Cup | 38-40 | 8-10 | 28-30 | 18-20 |
| Hot toddy or cider set; cookie jar, metal lid, metal tray, eight roly-poly glasses and ladle | 300-400 | — | — | — |
| Pitcher, 64 oz. (straight sides) | 275-300 | 65-75 | 150-175 | 110-125 |
| Pitcher, 8", 68 oz. | 300-350 | 85-95 | 225-250 | 125-150 |
| Pitcher, 8", 86 oz. | 350-400 | 100-125 | 285-300 | 150-175 |
| Pitcher, 8-1/2" | 500-600 | 85-95 | 200-225 | 200-225 |
| Plate, 6" | 15-18 | 6-8 | 12-15 | 10-12 |
| Plate, 8-1/2" | 40-45 | 10-12 | 20-24 | 20-24 |
| Plate, 10" | 40-45 | 20-22 | 35-40 | 30-35 |
| Plate, 9-7/8" (grill) | 35-40 | 12-15 | 28-30 | 22-24 |
| Platter, 13" (oval) | 65-75 | 24-26 | 45-50 | 40-45 |
| Salt and pepper (shakers, pair) | 300-350 | 50-60 | 150-175 | 75-85 |
| Saucer | 12-14 | 6-8 | 10-12 | 8-10 |
| Sherbet (footed) | 50-55 | 18-20 | 30-35 | 26-28 |
| Sherbet and detachable metal holder | 35-40 | 6-8 | — | — |
| Sugar | 60-65 | 12-15 | 30-35 | 22-24 |
| Sugar cover | 195-220 | 25-30 | 75-85 | 60-70 |
| Tumbler, 3-1/2" | 60-65 | 20-24 | 40-45 | 35-40 |
| Tumbler, 4-1/8" | 45-50 | 18-20 | 35-40 | 30-35 |
| Tumbler, 4-7/8" | 150-160 | 35-40 | 85-95 | 85-95 |
| Tumbler, 5-3/8" | 120-150 | 45-50 | 75-85 | 75-85 |

# ROYAL RUBY

## 1939-1967

Anchor-Hocking Glass Corporation

Lancaster, Pennsylvania

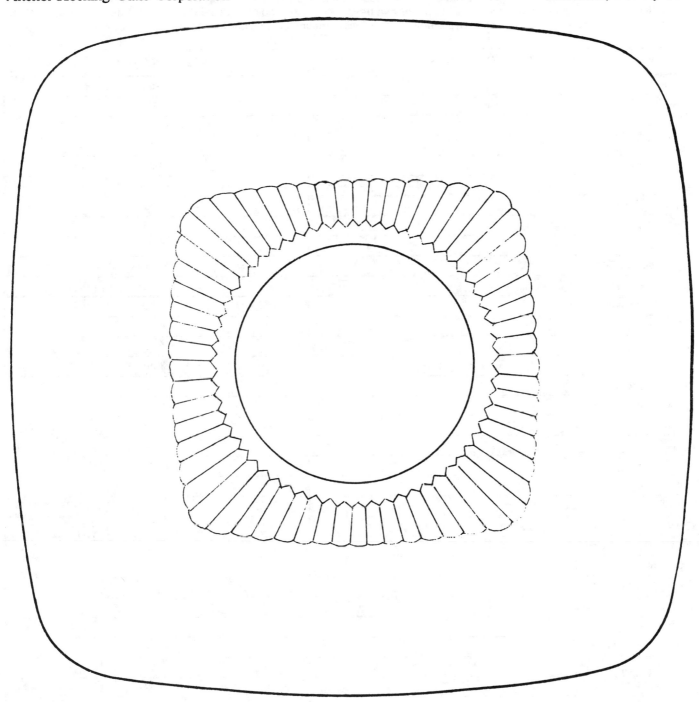

Colors found to date:

- Red only

# ROYAL RUBY

## Reproductions or reissues
Tumblers, 9 oz., 10 oz. and 13 oz.; Ball Vase.

## General pattern notes
Although Royal Ruby was meant originally by the company to describe color only, collectors use it as the name of this particular pattern. The company originally brought the pattern out in 1939-40. It is basically quite plain, except for the vibrant red color. Later (1950s), it introduced the squared pieces such as plates and trays. These newer pieces usually contained a center ribbed design. At the same time, it introduced the roly-poly type tumblers. You will sometimes find footed pieces with crystal bases.

| ITEM & DESCRIPTION | VALUE RANGES |
| --- | --- |
| Ashtray, 4-1/2" square | 6-8 |
| Bowl, 4-1/4" | 8-10 |
| Bowl, 5-1/4" | 10-12 |
| Bowl, 7-1/2" | 14-16 |
| Bowl, 8", oval | 18-20 |
| Bowl, 8-1/2" | 18-20 |
| Bowl, 10" deep | 30-35 |
| Bowl, 11-1/2" | 40-45 |
| Creamer, plain | 8-10 |
| Sugar, plain | 8-10 |
| Creamer, footed | 10-12 |
| Sugar, footed, covered | 18-20 |
| Cup, round or squared | 6-8 |
| Goblet | 10-12 |
| Pitcher, 22 oz., tilted | 28-30 |
| Pitcher, 22 oz., upright | 30-35 |
| Pitcher, 3 quart, tilted | 45-50 |
| Pitcher, 3 quart, upright | 65-75 |
| Plate, 6-1/2" | 4-6 |
| Plate, 7" | 8-10 |
| Plate, 7-3/4" | 8-10 |
| Plate, 9" | 14-16 |
| Plate, 13-3/4" | 45-50 |
| Punch bowl with stand | 100-125 |
| Saucer, round or squared | 3-4 |
| Sherbet, footed | 8-10 |
| Tumbler, 2-1/2 oz., footed | 6-8 |
| Tumbler, 3-1/2 oz. | 8-10 |
| Tumbler, 5 oz., 2 types | 8-10 |
| Tumbler, 9 oz. | 8-10 |
| Tumbler, 10 oz. | 10-12 |
| Tumbler, 13 oz. | 14-16 |
| Vase, ball type, 4" | 4-6 |
| Vase, 6-1/2" | 6-8 |
| Vase, assorted types and sizes | 18-24 |

# "S" PATTERN

## 1930 - 1933

Macbeth-Evans Glass Company                    Charleroi, Pennsylvania

Colors found to date:

- *Amber
- Green
- Blue
- Pink
- *Crystal (with and without color bands)
- Red
- *Yellow

# "S" PATTERN

**Reproductions or reissues**
None known to date.

**General pattern notes**
"S" Pattern is also known as "Stippled Rose Band." It is a busy, but beautiful, design. It is made particularly pretty to some collectors by the addition of bands of color in the rim-located stippled band design of the plates.

The three colors marked with an asterisk in the preceding list are the colors most likely to be found. Any others have to be considered quite rare and the value is what you're willing to pay.

| ITEM & DESCRIPTION | DOLLAR VALUE RANGES BY COLOR | |
| --- | --- | --- |
| | Crystal | Amber, Yellow, or Crystal (with color bands) |
| Bowl, 5-1/2" | 2-4 | 6-8 |
| Bowl, 8-1/2" | 8-10 | 16-18 |
| Creamer | 5-6 | 8-10 |
| Cup | 2-4 | 6-8 |
| Pitcher, 80 oz. | 45-50 | 100-125 |
| Plate, 6" | 1-2 | 3-4 |
| Plate, 8" | 2-3 | 5-6 |
| Plate, 9-1/4" | — | 8-10 |
| Plate (grill) | 4-6 | 6-8 |
| Plate, cake, 11" | 15-20 | 35-40 |
| Plate, cake, 13" | 35-40 | 65-75 |
| Saucer | 1-2 | 3-4 |
| Sherbet (footed) | 3-4 | 4-6 |
| Sugar | 5-6 | 8-10 |
| Tumbler, 3-1/2" | 5-6 | 6-8 |
| Tumbler, 4" | 4-6 | 8-10 |
| Tumbler, 4-1/4" | 4-6 | 8-10 |
| Tumbler, 5" | 6-8 | 10-12 |

# SANDWICH

## 1939 - 1964

Hocking Glass Company

(now Anchor-Hocking Glass Corporation)

Colors found to date:

- Amber
- Pink
- Crystal
- Red (Ruby)
- Green (Dark)
- White (Opaque)

# SANDWICH

## Reproductions or reissues

The company made its "Sandwich" pattern off and on throughout 25 years. Whether the collector wishes to call the later pieces reissues is up to individual discretion. The company did reissue the cookie jar, but it is larger than the original and easily identified by examining it. It made no cover for this reissue in green. The others do have covers.

## General pattern notes

Hocking first issued Sandwich in 1939-40, in green and ruby red, in a limited number of pieces, then sometime in the 1940s, it released a full line of crystal. Sometime after the crystal came some pink and ruby red. Then in the 1950s, it began producing more pieces in green and a small number of opaque white items. More green came in the late 1950s.

It is hard to determine whether Hocking produced all its colors continuously, but considering the amount of each available, one can surmise that most were.

Rarities in Hocking's Sandwich pattern include the small plate liner for the crystal custard; the pitchers, particularly the green ones; the butter dish and the cookie jar and cover; and bowls in green.

| ITEM & DESCRIPTION | DOLLAR VALUE RANGES BY COLOR | | | | |
|---|---|---|---|---|---|
| | Amber | Crystal | Green | Pink | Red |
| Bowl, 4-7/8" | 4-6 | 3-5 | 6-8 | 4-6 | 18-20 |
| Bowl, 5-1/4" | — | — | — | — | 18-20 |
| Bowl, 6" | 6-8 | 4-6 | — | — | — |
| Bowl, 6-1/2" | 6-8 | 4-6 | 30-35 | — | — |
| Bowl, 7" | — | 8-10 | 35-40 | — | — |
| Bowl, 8" | — | 8-10 | 35-40 | 20-24 | 45-50 |
| Bowl, 8-1/4" (oval) | — | 10-12 | — | — | — |
| Butter dish | — | 45-50 | — | — | — |
| Cookie jar and cover | 35-40 | 35-40 | 30-35 | — | — |
| Creamer | — | 6-8 | 18-20 | — | — |
| Cup | 2-4 | 2-4 | 18-20 | — | — |
| Custard cup | — | 3-4 | 4-6 | — | — |
| Custard cup liner | — | 10-12 | 6-8 | — | — |
| Pitcher, 6" | — | 45-50 | 145-160 | — | — |
| Pitcher, 2 quarts | — | 75-85 | 350-400 | — | — |
| Plate, 7" | — | 6-8 | 10-12 | — | — |
| Plate, 8" | — | 6-8 | — | — | — |
| Plate, 9" | 8-10 | 12-14 | 95-100 | — | — |
| Plate, 9" (ring for punch cup) | — | 6-8 | — | — | — |
| Plate, 12" | 18-20 | 18-20 | — | — | — |
| Punch bowl and stand | — | 40-45 | — | — | — |
| Punch cups | — | 3-4 | — | — | — |
| Saucer | 2-3 | 2-3 | 10-12 | — | — |
| Sherbet (footed) | — | 6-8 | — | — | — |
| Sugar and cover | — | 20-24 | 28-30 | — | — |
| Tumbler, 5 oz. | — | 6-8 | 4-6 | — | — |
| Tumbler, 9 oz. | — | 8-10 | 10-12 | — | — |
| Tumbler, 9 oz. (footed) | — | 28-30 | — | — | — |

# SANDWICH
1920 s to present

Indiana Glass Company

Dunkirk, Indiana

Colors found to date:

- Crystal
- Teal (Blue-Green)
- Green
- Red
- Pink

# SANDWICH

## Reproductions or reissues

This is a real bucket of worms. As with Hocking's Sandwich pattern, Indiana has been issuing various items and colors periodically over the years. The problem with this is that the company is still producing its Sandwich today. This is even further complicated by its production of several items for exclusive distribution through Tiara home-party sales.

## General pattern notes

The listing of values below is useful for all the colors, but use the values for crystal with caution. The market is very unstable to the down side presently and the values reflect that, but they can vary quite widely with dealers.

There are few reliable ways to distinguish old from new in Indiana's Sandwich pattern. The problem is that this applies to only two or three items. For instance, if you pick up a cup, a creamer, or a sugar bowl and see the 1933 World's Fair inscription, then you know.

| ITEM & DESCRIPTION | DOLLAR VALUE RANGES BY COLOR | | | |
|---|---|---|---|---|
| | Crystal | Green or Pink | Red | Teal (Blue) |
| Ashtray set | | | | |
| (clubs, spades, hearts, diamonds) | 4-6 | 6-8 | — | — |
| Bowl, 4-1/4" | 3-4 | 4-6 | — | — |
| Bowl, 6" | 4-5 | — | — | — |
| Bowl, 6" (six sides) | 4-5 | — | — | 14-16 |
| Bowl, 8-1/4" | 10-12 | 8-10 | — | — |
| Bowl, 9" (console) | 10-12 | 14-16 | — | — |
| Bowl, 10" (console) | 12-14 | 18-20 | — | — |
| Butter dish and cover | 24-28 | 145-160 | — | 160-175 |
| Candlesticks, 3-1/2" (pair) | 14-16 | 28-30 | — | — |
| Candlesticks, 7" (pair) | 28-30 | 40-45 | — | — |
| Creamer | 6-8 | 8-10 | — | — |
| Cruet and stopper | 24-26 | — | — | 120-130 |
| Cup | 3-5 | 5-6 | 24-26 | 10-12 |
| Creamer and sugar (on diamond-shaped tray) | 18-20 | — | — | 28-30 |
| Decanter and stopper | 24-26 | 85-95 | — | — |
| Goblet, 9 oz. | 14-16 | 16-18 | — | — |
| Pitcher | 36-38 | 85-95 | — | — |
| Plate, 6" | 2-4 | 4-6 | — | 6-8 |
| Plate, 7" | 4-5 | — | — | — |
| Plate, 8" (ringed off-center for sherbet) | 4-5 | 8-10 | — | 10-12 |
| Plate, 8-3/8" | 4-5 | 6-8 | — | — |
| Plate, 10-1/2" | 8-10 | 24-26 | — | — |
| Plate, 13" | 14-16 | 20-24 | — | — |
| Sandwich server (center handled) | 18-20 | 24-28 | — | — |
| Saucer | 1-2 | 3-4 | 6-8 | 4-5 |
| Sherbet | 4-6 | 6-8 | — | 8-10 |
| Sugar (no cover) | 4-6 | 6-8 | 35-45 | — |
| Tumbler, 3 oz. (footed) | 6-8 | 10-12 | — | — |
| Tumbler, 8 oz. (footed) | 8-10 | 14-16 | — | — |
| Tumbler, 12 oz. (footed) | 8-10 | 14-16 | — | — |
| Wine, 3" | 6-8 | 18-20 | — | — |

# SHARON

### 1931 - 1933

Federal Glass Company

Columbus, Ohio

**Colors found to date:**

- Amber
- Crystal
- Green
- Pink

# SHARON

## Reproductions or reissues

There have been reproductions of six items found in the Sharon pattern: shakers, covered butter, cheese dishes, candy dishes, sugars, and creamers.

The salt and pepper shakers are poorly made, as is the case of most of the reproductions. The pattern is the same, but the leaves and flowers are not rendered very well. The roses don't look like roses, as in the original.

In the genuine pattern, covers for butter and cheese dishes are identical. So it is with the reproductions. The same problems exhibited on the shaker reproductions apply to the covers; however, the knob on top is the chief giveaway on the reproduction. On the reproduction, the knob is easily grasped, while on the old original, the knob is flatter and there is little space between the bottom of the knob and the top of the cover, making it hard to grasp. So, if you can pick up the top easily, beware.

The butter and cheese dishes themselves are thicker than the originals and have an overall awkward look. The ridge upon which the cover sits is more sharply defined and higher on the reproduction than on the original.

The colors and reproductions have been found so far in blue, dark and light green, a color somewhat like topaz, but reddish-brown, and pink.

## General pattern notes

"Sharon" has been called "Cabbage Rose" in the past.

Although you will see crystal in the color list, there is too little of it around to be able to price it with any authority, so it doesn't appear in the value list below. Don't make the mistake of thinking crystal more valuable because of this. Crystal, in fact, is considerably less. A good guideline would be to price it at about one-fourth the values listed for amber pieces.

Rarities are the covered cheese, covered butter dish, the salt and pepper shaker pair, and green footed 6-1/2-inch tumblers.

| ITEM & DESCRIPTION | DOLLAR VALUE RANGES BY COLOR | | |
|---|---|---|---|
| | Amber | Green | Pink |
| Bowl, 5" | 8-10 | 16-18 | 14-15 |
| Bowl, 5" (cream soup) | 28-30 | 55-60 | 45-50 |
| Bowl, 6" | 22-24 | 28-30 | 28-30 |
| Bowl, 7-1/2" | 52-55 | — | 55-60 |
| Bowl, 8-1/2" | 5-6 | 35-38 | 30-35 |
| Bowl, 9-1/2" (oval) | 20-22 | 35-38 | 35-38 |
| Bowl, 10-1/2" | 24-26 | 40-45 | 40-45 |
| Butter dish and cover | 45-50 | 95-110 | 60-65 |
| Cake plate, 11-1/2" (footed) | 20-24 | 60-65 | 40-45 |
| Candy jar and cover | 45-50 | 145-160 | 60-65 |
| Cheese dish and cover | 195-225 | — | 1200-1400 |
| Creamer (footed) | 12-14 | 20-24 | 18-20 |
| Cup | 8-10 | 18-20 | 12-14 |
| Jam dish, 7-1/2" | 40-45 | 65-75 | 200-225 |
| Pitcher, 80 oz. (ice lip) | 145-165 | 400-450 | 175-185 |
| Pitcher, 80 oz. | 140-150 | 475-500 | 175-185 |
| Plate, 6" | 4-5 | 6-8 | 6-8 |
| Plate, 7-1/2" | 15-18 | 18-20 | 24-26 |
| Plate, 9-1/2" | 10-12 | 24-26 | 18-20 |
| Platter, 12-1/2" (oval) | 18-20 | 32-35 | 30-32 |
| Salt and pepper (shakers, pair) | 35-40 | 65-70 | 60-70 |
| Saucer | 4-5 | 8-10 | 8-10 |
| Sherbet (footed) | 12-14 | 34-36 | 16-18 |
| Sugar and cover | 28-30 | 60-65 | 45-50 |
| Tumbler, 4-1/8" | 30-35 | 65-75 | 45-50 |
| Tumbler, 5-1/4" (thin walled) | 50-55 | 100-120 | 50-55 |
| Tumbler, 5-1/4" (thick walled) | 60-65 | 100-110 | 85-95 |
| Tumbler, 6-1/2" (footed) | 125-145 | — | 60-65 |

# SIERRA
## 1931 - 1933

Jeannette Glass Company

Jeannette, Pennsylvania

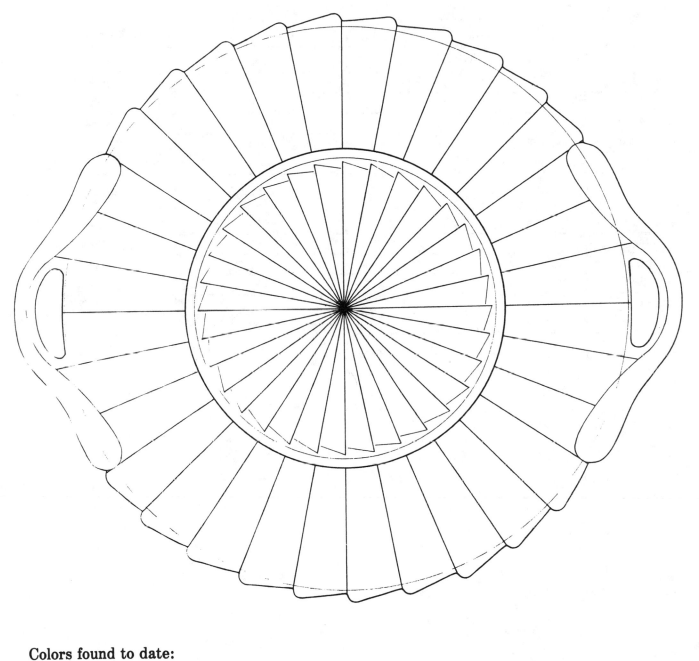

**Colors found to date:**

• Green          • Pink

# SIERRA

**Reproductions or reissues**

None known to date.

**General pattern notes**

Sierra was not in production long. Jeannette discontinued it because of the tendency of the points of the serrated edge to be easily broken. The pattern is moderately scarce because of the short production time. This pattern is also sometimes known as "Plnwheel."

Pitchers, tumblers, and covered butter dishes are among the items most difficult to obtain in Sierra. The combination Adam-Sierra design butter dish cover is coveted by collectors.

| ITEM & DESCRIPTION | DOLLAR VALUE RANGES BY COLOR | |
|---|---|---|
| | Green | Pink |
| Bowl, 5-1/2" | 16-18 | 14-16 |
| Bowl, 8-1/2" | 38-40 | 38-40 |
| Bowl, 9-1/4" (oval) | 135-145 | 65-75 |
| Butter dish and cover | 85-95 | 75-85 |
| Creamer | 20-24 | 20-22 |
| Cup | 14-16 | 12-14 |
| Pitcher, 6-1/2" | 145-150 | 110-120 |
| Plate, 9" | 26-28 | 24-26 |
| Platter, 11" (oval) | 60-70 | 50-60 |
| Salt and pepper (shaker, pair) | 50-55 | 45-50 |
| Saucer | 6-8 | 8-10 |
| Serving tray (two-handled) | 24-26 | 22-24 |
| Sugar and cover | 45-50 | 40-45 |
| Tumbler, 4-1/2" (footed) | 75-85 | 55-65 |

# SPIRAL

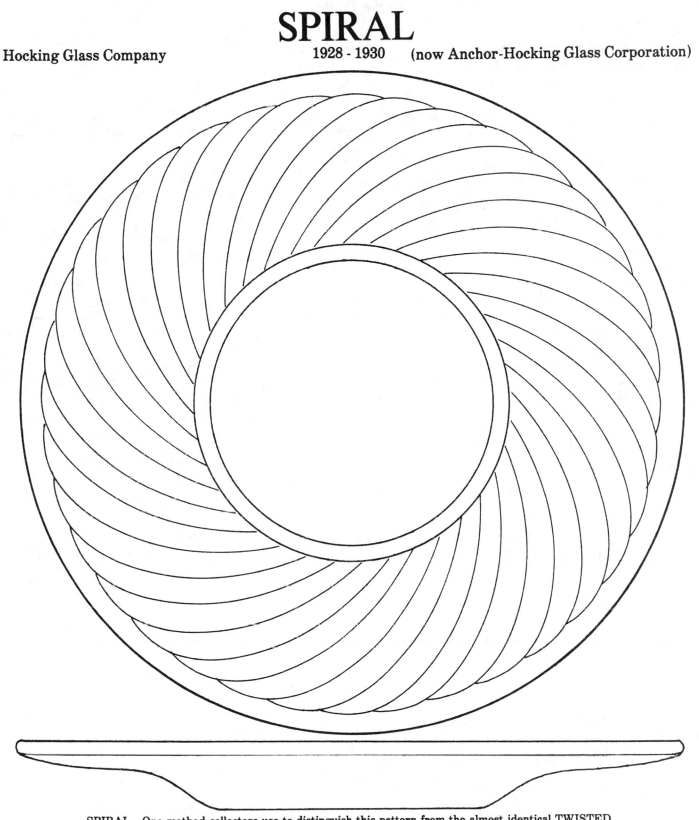

SPIRAL. One method collectors use to distinguish this pattern from the almost identical TWISTED OPTIC pattern is by the differing direction orientation of the spirals. As you can see the spirals are oriented in a clockwise direction here and those on the TWISTED OPTIC pieces are counterclockwise. This is so in the majority of the cases but not always. A more reliable way to tell the difference is to turn the plates over and examine the base. As you can see by the cross-section drawing here, the base flares out evenly from the bottom. If you will turn to the TWISTED OPTIC cross-section drawing you will be able to readily discern the difference.

# SPIRAL

## Colors found to date
Green—and crystal is shown in an old catalog, but it is not known if any is in collectors' hands.

## Reproductions or reissues
None known to date.

## General pattern notes
Spiral is all too easily confused with Imperial's "Twisted Optic" pattern. The only reliable way to know the difference is to experience it. You should physically handle each if you have the opportunity. There are some unreliable methods based upon which way the spirals go, right or left.

Collecting this pattern is an inexpensive way to get started in Depression glass.

| ITEM & DESCRIPTION | DOLLAR VALUE RANGES BY COLOR |
| --- | --- |
| | Green |
| Bowl, 4-3/4" | 5-6 |
| Bowl, 7" | 10-12 |
| Bowl, 8" | 12-14 |
| Creamer (flat or footed) | 6-8 |
| Cup | 5-6 |
| Ice or butter tub | 30-35 |
| Pitcher, 7-5/8" | 40-45 |
| Plate, 6" | 4-5 |
| Plate, 8" | 5-6 |
| Preserve and cover | 40-45 |
| Salt and pepper (shaker, pair) | 45-50 |
| Sandwich server (center handled) | 20-24 |
| Saucer | 2-3 |
| Sherbet | 4-5 |
| Sugar (flat or footed) | 6-8 |
| Tumbler, 3" | 6-8 |
| Tumbler, 5" | 16-18 |

# STARLIGHT

### 1938 - 1940

Hazel Atlas Glass Company

Clarksburg, West Virginia and Zanesville, Ohio

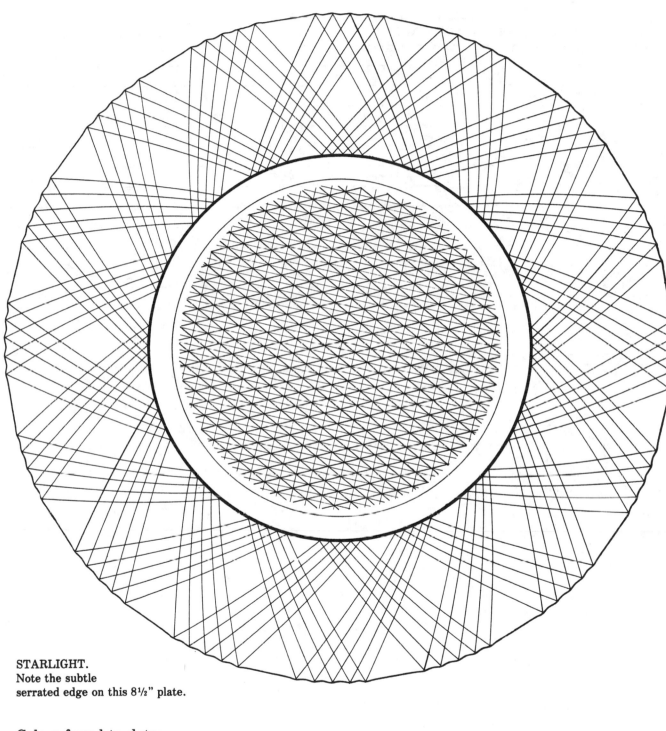

**STARLIGHT.**
Note the subtle
serrated edge on this 8½" plate.

Colors found to date:

- Blue (Cobalt)    - Crystal    - Pink    - White (Opaque)

# STARLIGHT

**Reproductions or reissues**

None known to date.

**General pattern notes**

The blue pieces seem to be available in limited numbers. The pattern is striking, but the values remain curiously low.

| ITEM & DESCRIPTION | DOLLAR VALUE RANGES BY COLOR |
| --- | --- |
| | All colors |
| Bowl, 5-1/2" | 8-12 |
| Bowl, 4-3/4" | 8-10 |
| Bowl, 8-1/2" (closed handle) | 10-20 |
| *Bowl, 11-1/2", salad | 20-24 |
| Creamer (oval) | 3-4 |
| Cup | 6-8 |
| Plate, 6" | 5-6 |
| Plate, 8-1/2" | 4-5 |
| Plate, 9" | 8-10 |
| Plate, 13" | 15-18 |
| Relish dish | 10-12 |
| Salt and pepper (shaker, pair) | 22-24 |
| Saucer | 2-3 |
| Sherbet | 8-10 |
| Sugar (oval) | 6-8 |
| *There was a metal base designed for this bowl. | |

# STRAWBERRY

c. 1930

U. S. Glass Company

Pittsburgh, Pennsylvania

Colors found to date:

- Crystal
- Green
- Pink

# STRAWBERRY

**Reproductions or reissues**

None known to date.

**General pattern notes**

"Strawberry" is occasionally found with the same pattern design, but with cherries instead of strawberries. These pieces so far are the butter dish cover, the tumbler, and pitcher. Pieces with the cherries are called "Cherryberry" by dealers and collectors. Their values generally run slightly higher than the regular pieces in pink or green.

Pitchers and covered butter dishes are the plums in this pattern. The butter dish covers have the same design motif, but the dishes themselves have only a center rayed design, no berries.

| ITEM & DESCRIPTION | DOLLAR VALUE RANGES BY COLOR | |
| --- | --- | --- |
| | Crystal or Iridescent | Green or Pink |
| Bowl, 4" | 5-6 | 15-18 |
| Bowl, 6-1/4" | 20-24 | 100-120 |
| Bowl, 6-1/2" | 12-14 | 24-26 |
| Bowl, 7-1/2" | 18-20 | 30-35 |
| Butter dish and cover | 125-135 | 195-220 |
| Compote, 5-3/4" | 12-14 | 24-26 |
| Creamer (small) | 8-10 | 22-24 |
| Creamer, 4-5/8" | 15-18 | 30-35 |
| Olive dish, 5" (one-handled) | 8-10 | 18-20 |
| Pickle dish, 8-1/4" (oval) | 8-10 | 20-24 |
| Pitcher, 7-3/4" | 165-175 | 200-225 |
| Plate, 6" | 4-5 | 10-12 |
| Plate, 7-1/2" | 8-10 | 16-18 |
| Sherbet | 6-8 | 8-10 |
| Sugar (small, no cover) | 15-18 | 22-24 |
| Sugar (large, covered) | 28-30 | 95-110 |
| Tumbler, 3-5/8" | 10-12 | 32-34 |

# SUNFLOWER

c. 1930

Jeannette Glass Company

Jeannette, Pennsylvania

**Colors found to date:**

- *Delphite
- Green
- Pink

*Very rare. Insufficient data to establish realistic values at present.

# SUNFLOWER

**Reproductions and reissues**

None known to date.

**General pattern notes**

The rarest piece in the Sunflower pattern is the 7-inch trivet or hot plate. It has three legs and a raised edge. The cake plate is the most commonly found item.

| ITEM & DESCRIPTION | DOLLAR VALUE RANGES BY COLOR |
| --- | --- |
| | Green or Pink |
| Ashtray, 5" (center design only) | 10-12 |
| Cake plate, 10" (three-legged) | 20-24 |
| Creamer (opaque: 72-87) | 22-24 |
| Cup | 14-16 |
| Hot plate or trivet, 7" | 350-450 |
| Plate, 9" | 24-26 |
| Saucer | 8-10 |
| Sugar (opaque: 72-87) | 22-24 |
| Tumbler, 4-3/4" (footed) | 35-40 |

# SWIRL
### 1937 - 1938

Jeannette Glass Company

Jeannette, Pennsylvania

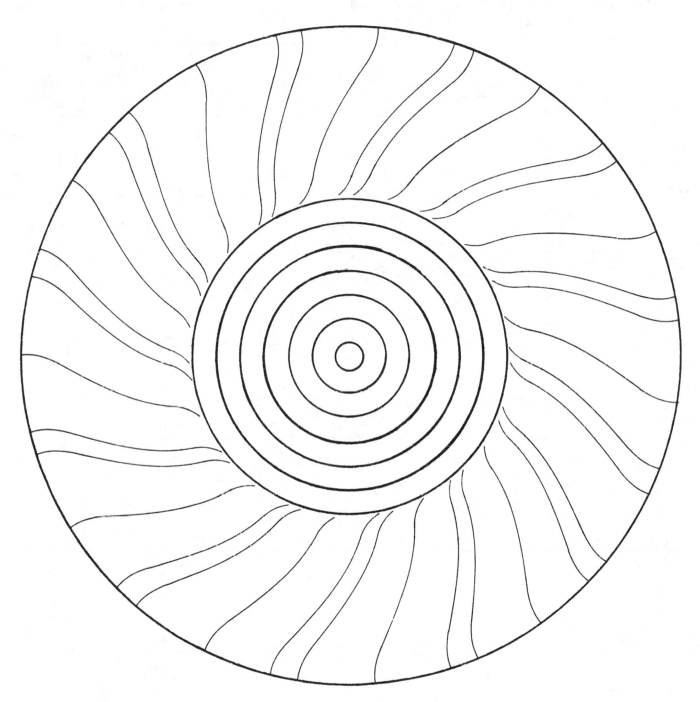

**Colors found to date:**

- Amber
  - Pink
- Blue
  - Aquamarine (Green-Blue)
- Delphite

# SWIRL

**Reproductions or reissues**

None known to date.

**General pattern notes**

"Swirl" has been referred to as "Petal Swirl" also.

Very little delphite was made and acquiring the covered butter dishes will be painful to the pocketbook, with the covered candy dish running into a sizable outlay as well. Blue and amber anything would be a nice catch.

| ITEM & DESCRIPTION | DOLLAR VALUE RANGES BY COLOR | | |
|---|---|---|---|
| | Delphite | Pink | Ultramarine |
| Ashtray | — | 8-10 | — |
| Bowl, 5-1/4" | 14-16 | 12-14 | 14-16 |
| Bowl, 10" (footed, with handles) | 28-30 | 22-24 | 30-32 |
| Bowl, console, 10-1/2" (footed) | — | 30-35 | 30-35 |
| Butter dish and cover | — | 24-28 | 30-35 |
| Candleholders (double, pair) | — | 210-225 | 275-295 |
| Candleholders (single, pair) | — | 60-70 | 50-60 |
| Candy dish (no cover, three-legged) | 125-150 | — | — |
| Candy dish with cover | — | 14-16 | 18-20 |
| Coaster | — | 160-175 | 150-160 |
| Creamer (footed) | — | 14-16 | 16-18 |
| Cup | 10-12 | 14-16 | 14-16 |
| Pitcher (footed) | 8-10 | 10-12 | 14-16 |
| Plate, 6-1/2" | — | — | 1,600-1,800 |
| Plate, 7-1/4" | 6-8 | 6-8 | 8-10 |
| Plate, 8" | — | 8-10 | 14-16 |
| Plate, 9-1/4" | 12-15 | 16-18 | 12-14 |
| Plate, 10-1/2" | 12-15 | 18-20 | 20-22 |
| Plate, 12-1/2" | 24-26 | — | — |
| Platter, 12" (oval) | 38-40 | — | — |
| Salt and pepper (shaker, pair) | — | — | 45-50 |
| Saucer | 4-5 | 3-4 | 5-6 |
| Sherbet (footed) | — | 18-20 | 22-25 |
| Soup (handled) | — | 35-38 | 45-50 |
| Sugar (footed) | 10-12 | 14-16 | 14-16 |
| Tumbler, 4" | — | 22-24 | 34-36 |
| Tumbler, 4-5/8" | — | 24-26 | 45-50 |
| Tumbler, 4-3/4" | — | 50-60 | 120-130 |
| Tumbler, 9 oz. (footed) | — | 24-26 | 45-50 |
| Vase, 6-1/2" (footed) | — | 26-28 | — |
| Vase, 8-1/2" (footed) | — | — | 28-30 |

# TEA ROOM
## 1926 - 1931

Indiana Glass Company

Dunkirk, Indiana

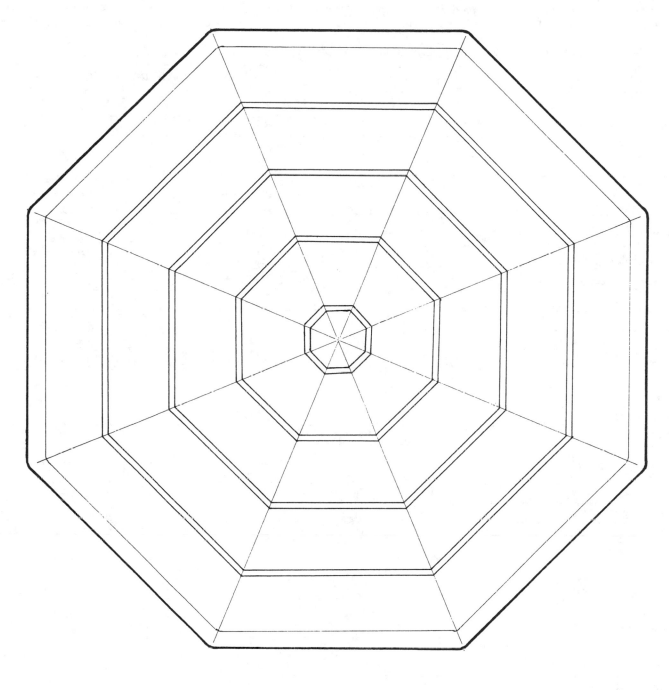

Colors found to date:

- Amber
- Crystal
- Green
- Pink

# TEAROOM

**Reproductions or reissues**

None known to date.

**General pattern notes**

This pattern line is quite large and has a great variety of items in it. For instance, there are at least seven different sizes and styles of tumblers.

In spite of the size of the line and its production being primarily for soda fountains and tea rooms, little of it seems to have survived the years. It is also difficult to locate mint items. It is heavy, but angular and sharp edged in design, so it was subject to much chipping when handled or washed.

Anything found in amber, and the pitcher in crystal, will bring a premium price.

| ITEM & DESCRIPTION | DOLLAR VALUE RANGES BY COLOR |
| --- | --- |
| | Green or Pink |
| Bowl, 7-1/2" (banana split, footed) | 75-85 |
| Bowl, 8-1/2" | 30-35 |
| Bowl, 8-3/4" | 75-85 |
| Bowl, 9-1/2" (oval) | 65-75 |
| Candlestick (pair) | 55-65 |
| Creamer, 4" | 30-35 |
| Creamer, 4-1/2" (footed) | 20-25 |
| Creamer (rectangular) | 20-25 |
| Creamer and sugar with tray, 3-1/2" | 75-85 |
| Cup | 50-60 |
| Electric lamp | 125-135 |
| Goblet | 70-80 |
| Ice tub | 60-70 |
| Mustard with cover | 150-175 |
| Parfait | 85-95 |
| Pitcher | 175-185 |
| Plate, 6-1/2" | 35-40 |
| Plate, 8-1/4" | 35-40 |
| Plate, 10-1/2" (two-handled) | 45-50 |
| Relish (sectioned) | 26-28 |
| Salt and pepper (shaker, pair) | 75-85 |
| Saucer | 25-30 |
| Sherbets (three styles) | 30-40 |
| Sugar, 4" | 30-35 |
| Sugar, 4-1/2" (footed) | 20-25 |
| Sugar (rectangular) | 20-25 |
| Sugar and cover | 75-85 |
| Sundae (footed) | 75-85 |
| Tumbler, 8-1/2" | 50-60 |
| Tumbler, 6 oz. (footed) | 50-60 |
| Tumbler, 9 oz. (footed) | 55-65 |
| Tumbler, 11 oz. (footed) | 50-60 |
| Tumbler, 12 oz. (footed) | 65-75 |
| Vase, 6" | 90-100 |
| Vase, 9" | 85-95 |
| Vase, 11" | 135-145 |

# THISTLE

c. 1930

Macbeth-Evans Glass Company                    Charleroi, Pennsylvania

Colors found to date:

- Crystal          - Green          - Pink          - *Yellow

*In very short supply.  Not often found.

# THISTLE

**Reproductions or reissues**

None known to date.

**General pattern notes**

Pink is the more prevalent color available, but know that the pattern is fairly hard to find in any color.

The large pink bowl is the prize in this pattern, but the pitcher and cake plate are both highly desirable in any color.

| ITEM & DESCRIPTION | DOLLAR VALUE RANGES BY COLOR | |
| --- | --- | --- |
| | Green | Pink |
| Bowl, 5-1/2" | 28-30 | 26-28 |
| Bowl, 10-1/4" | 240-250 | 350-400 |
| Cup | 26-28 | 24-26 |
| Plate, 8" | 22-24 | 20-22 |
| Plate, 10-1/4" (grill) | 30-35 | 30-35 |
| Plate, cake, 13" | 165-175 | 140-160 |
| Saucer | 10-12 | 8-10 |

# THUMBPRINT

**1927 - 1930**

Federal Glass Company                                    Columbus, Ohio

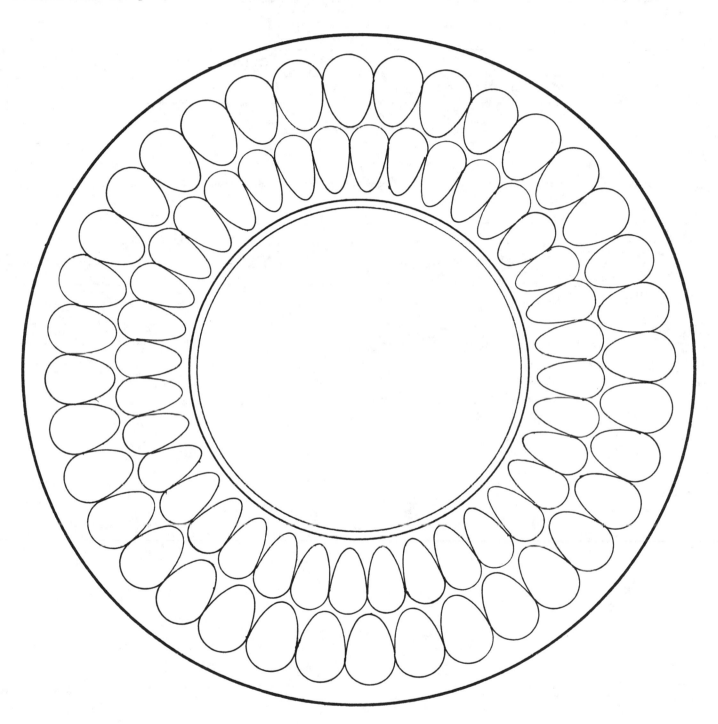

Colors found to date:     • Green only

# THUMBPRINT

**Reproductions or reissues**

None known to date.

**General pattern notes**

This pattern was made primarily for promotional giveaways in cups and saucers.

"Thumbprint" is easily confused with the company's similar "Raindrops" pattern. Please turn back to Page 168 for an explanation of the differences.

The sugar bowl and creamer are scarce.

| ITEM & DESCRIPTION | DOLLAR VALUE RANGES BY COLOR |
| --- | --- |
| | Green |
| Bowl, 4-3/4" | 10-12 |
| Bowl, 5" | 10-12 |
| Bowl, 8" | 18-20 |
| Creamer (footed) | 10-12 |
| Cup | 6-8 |
| Plate, 6" | 8-10 |
| Plate, 8" | 12-14 |
| Plate, 9-1/4" | 18-20 |
| Salt and pepper (shaker, pair) | 65-75 |
| Saucer | 1-2 |
| Sherbet | 6-8 |
| Sugar (footed) | 10-12 |
| Tumbler, 4" | 16-18 |
| Tumbler, 5" | 18-20 |
| Tumbler, 5-1/2" | 24-26 |
| Whiskey jigger, 2-1/4" | 10-12 |

# TWISTED OPTIC
## 1927 - 1930

**Imperial Glass Company**                                          **Bellaire, Ohio**

TWISTED OPTIC. This is a cross-section drawing of a plate showing the distinctive shape of the base in TWISTED OPTIC plates. The overall pattern design is identical to that of SPIRAL except for this base and that the majority of TWISTED OPTIC items have a counter clockwise spiraling. The SPIRAL pattern items are oriented in a clockwise direction. This latter observation is not always so making it a bit unreliable as a positive identification characteristic.

## Colors found to date:

- Amber
- *Blue
- Green
- Pink
- *Yellow

# TWISTED OPTIC

**Reproductions or reissues**
　None known to date.

**General pattern notes**
　Be careful not to confuse this pattern with Hocking's "Spiral." Please refer back to "Spiral" for discussion of how to tell the difference.
　*Matched sherbets and ringed plates have been found, but they are presently too unique to assign a realistic value.

| ITEM & DESCRIPTION | DOLLAR VALUE RANGES BY COLOR |
|---|---|
| | All color |
| Bowl, 4-3/4" | 10-12 |
| Bowl, 5" | 6-8 |
| Bowl, 7" | 8-10 |
| Bowl, console, 10-1/2" | 26-28 |
| Bowl, console, 11-1/2" | 15-25 |
| Candlesticks, 3" (pair) | 24-30 |
| Candy jar and cover | 45-60 |
| Candy jar and cover (footed) | 60-70 |
| Creamer | 6-8 |
| Cup | 6-8 |
| Pitcher | 35-45 |
| Plate, 6" | 4-5 |
| Plate, 7" | 6-8 |
| Plate, 7-1/2" x 9" (oval) | 8-12 |
| Plate, 8" | 6-8 |
| Powder box with cover | 35-50 |
| Preserve (same as candy jar, but with slot in lid for server) | 65-75 |
| Sandwich server (center handled) | 18-20 |
| Sandwich server (two-handled) | 12-15 |
| Saucer | 1-2 |
| Sherbet | 6-8 |
| Sugar | 6-8 |
| Tumbler, 4-1/2" | 10-12 |
| Tumbler, 5-1/4" | 12-14 |

# VERNON (No. 616)

**1930 - 1933**

**Indiana Glass Company**                                    **Dunkirk, Indiana**

**Colors found to date:**

- Crystal          - Green          - Yellow

# VERNON (No. 616)

## Reproductions or reissues
None known to date.

## General pattern notes
This is a very difficult pattern of Depression glass to find. There are few pieces to be collected when you do find it. The crystal pieces are becoming scarce, but the green still commands the higher prices.

| ITEM & DESCRIPTION | DOLLAR VALUE RANGES BY COLOR | | |
|---|---|---|---|
| | Crystal | Green | Yellow |
| Bowl, 4-1/2" | 3-6 | 5-7 | 4-6 |
| Bowl, 6-1/2" | 4-7 | 4-8 | 4-7 |
| Bowl, 7-1/2" | 6-9 | 7-10 | 8-10 |
| Bowl, 9" | 8-11 | 11-16 | 11-16 |
| Creamer (footed) | 8-10 | 20-24 | 24-26 |
| Cup | 6-8 | 16-18 | 18-20 |
| Pitcher, 8-1/2" | 32-42 | 50-70 | 48-68 |
| Plate, 8" | 4-5 | 8-10 | 10-12 |
| Plate, 11" | 8-10 | 24-26 | 24-26 |
| Plate (grill) | 6-9 | 8-12 | 8-12 |
| Saucer | 1-2 | 3-4 | 3-4 |
| Sugar (footed) | 8-10 | 20-24 | 24-26 |
| Tumbler (small, footed) | 6-8 | 8-10 | 10-12 |
| Tumbler (medium, footed) | 8-10 | 10-12 | 12-14 |
| Tumbler (large, footed) | 10-12 | 12-14 | 14-16 |

# VICTORY
### 1929 - 1930 s

Diamond Glass-Ware Company                    Indiana, Pennsylvania

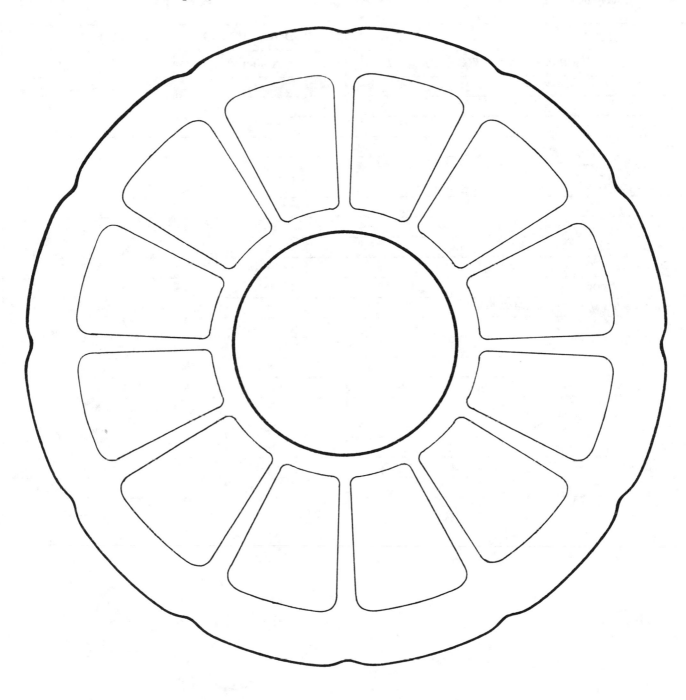

Colors found to date:

- Amber
- Green
- Black
- Pink
- *Blue (Cobalt)

*Too unique to price. No trade data found.

# VICTORY

**Reproductions or reissues**

None known to date.

**General pattern notes**

The blue pieces are very hard to come by. There have been a few pieces found that were elaborately decorated in gold, and some vessels have gold rims.

| ITEM & DESCRIPTION | DOLLAR VALUE RANGES BY COLOR | |
| --- | --- | --- |
| | Amber | Green or Pink |
| Bowl, 6-1/2" | 10-12 | 14-16 |
| Bowl, 8-1/2" | 18-20 | 22-24 |
| Bowl, 9" (oval) | 26-28 | 30-32 |
| Bowl, console, 12" | 30-32 | 36-28 |
| Candlesticks, 3" (pair) | 35-40 | 50-60 |
| Cheese and cracker set, 12" (indented plate and compote) | — | 45-50 |
| Compote, 6" | 12-14 | 16-18 |
| Creamer | 8-10 | 10-12 |
| Cup | 8-10 | 10-12 |
| Goblet, 5" | 16-18 | 22-24 |
| Gravy boat (with drip plate) | 35-45 | 65-75 |
| Mayonnaise set, 3-1/2" (includes 8-1/2" indented plate with a ladle) | 40-45 | 50-60 |
| Plate, 6" | 4-6 | 10-12 |
| Plate, 7" | 6-8 | 12-14 |
| Plate, 8" | 8-10 | 14-16 |
| Plate, 9" | 16-18 | 30-35 |
| Platter, 12" | 24-26 | 30-35 |
| Sandwich server (center handled) | 28-30 | 30-35 |
| Saucer | 3-4 | 5-6 |
| Sherbet (footed) | 10-12 | 12-14 |
| Sugar | 8-10 | 10-12 |

# WATERFORD

1938 - 1944, 1950 s

Hocking Glass Company

(now Anchor-Hocking Glass Corporation)

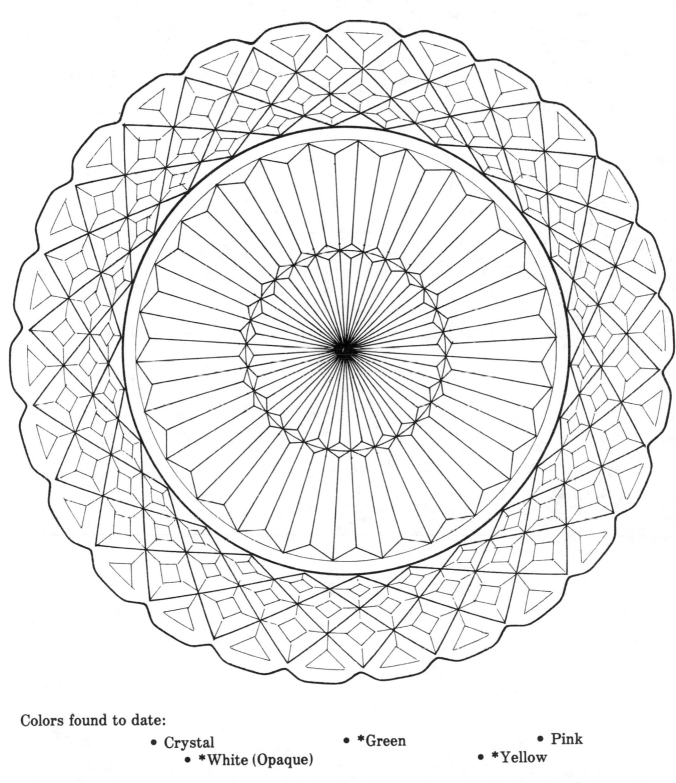

Colors found to date:

- Crystal
- *Green
- Pink
- *White (Opaque)
- *Yellow

*Items in this color only occasionally turn up. No trade data, so no values can be realistically assigned to them.

# WATERFORD

## Reproductions or reissues

In the mid- and late 1950s, the company modified the old 13-1/2-inch sandwich plate and produced a relish set. It consisted of a five-section plate with a small cup-like dish to be placed in the center, surrounded by inserts made in colors contrasting with the plate: red inserts with crystal and ivory inserts with a green plate. In addition, it released the 5-1/4-inch goblet in crystal.

## General pattern notes

Once called "Waffle," this pattern was first produced by Hocking in 1938 in pink and phased out rather quickly, offering only occasional pieces in pink. Then, the following year, it introduced a full line of tableware in crystal and added accessory pieces through the years until 1944. The green, white, and yellow pieces may have been color experiments or whims of factory workers. In any case, they are not often found.

| ITEM & DESCRIPTION | DOLLAR VALUE RANGES BY COLOR | |
| --- | --- | --- |
| | Crystal | Pink |
| Ashtray | 6-8 | — |
| Bowl, 4-3/4" | 6-8 | 14-16 |
| Bowl, 5-1/2" | 16-18 | 28-30 |
| Bowl, 8-1/4" | 12-14 | 20-24 |
| Butter dish and cover | 30-35 | 200-225 |
| Coaster, 4" | 4-5 | — |
| Creamer (oval) | 4-5 | 10-12 |
| Cup | 6-8 | 16-18 |
| Goblet, 5-1/4" | 16-18 | — |
| Goblet, 5-5/8" | 16-18 | — |
| Lamp, 4" (rounded base) | 30-35 | — |
| Pitcher, 42 oz. (tilted) | 28-30 | — |
| Pitcher, 80 oz. (tilted) | 40-45 | 165-175 |
| Plate, 6" | 4-5 | 8-10 |
| Plate, 7-1/8" | 6-8 | 12-15 |
| Plate, 9-5/8" | 12-14 | 26-28 |
| Plate, cake, 10-1/4" (handled) | 10-12 | 18-24 |
| Plate, sandwich, 13-3/4" | 12-15 | 26-28 |
| Relish, 13-3/4" (5-sectioned) | 18-20 | — |
| Salt and pepper (2 styles) | 10-12 | — |
| Saucer | 3-5 | 6-8 |
| Sherbet (footed, 2 styles) | 4-5 | 14-16 |
| Sugar and cover | 16-18 | 45-55 |
| Tumbler, 3-1/2" | — | 85-95 |
| Tumbler, 4-7/8" (footed) | 10-12 | 25-30 |

# WINDSOR
### 1936 - 1946

**Jeannette Glass Company**                    **Jeannette, Pennsylvania**

Colors found to date:

- Crystal          - Delphite          - Green
  - Pink                    - Red

# WINDSOR

**Reproductions or reissues**

None known to date.

**General pattern notes**

When Windsor was first released in 1936, it was a large line and only made in pink and green. In 1937, the company apparently stopped production of the green and added crystal. That would explain the shortage of green items.

Candleholders are hard to find in pink.

An unusual boat-shaped (pointed at each end) bowl was produced, but it is not remarkably priced and is nice to have in any collection of Windsor.

The delphite and red pieces turn up very infrequently. There has been insufficient trade data to establish realistic values for these colors.

| ITEM & DESCRIPTION | DOLLAR VALUE RANGES BY COLOR | | |
|---|---|---|---|
| | Crystal | Green | Pink |
| Ashtray, 5-3/4" | 18-20 | 40-45 | 40-42 |
| Bowl, 4-3/4" | 4-5 | 10-12 | 10-12 |
| Bowl, 5" | — | — | 24-26 |
| Bowl, 5" (cream soup) | 6-8 | 28-30 | 24-26 |
| Bowl, 5-1/8" | 8-10 | 24-26 | 22-24 |
| Bowl, 5-3/8" | 8-10 | 24-26 | 22-24 |
| Bowl, 7-1/8" (3-legged) | 8-10 | — | 30-35 |
| Bowl, 8" | 12-15 | — | 50-60 |
| Bowl, 8" (2-handled) | 8-10 | 22-24 | 24-26 |
| Bowl, 8-1/2" | 8-10 | 22-24 | 24-26 |
| Bowl, 9-1/2" (oval) | 8-10 | 28-30 | 26-28 |
| Bowl, 10-1/2" (blunted points on scalloped edge) | 24-26 | — | — |
| Bowl, 10-1/2" (sharp points on scalloped edge) | — | — | 110-125 |
| Bowl, console, 12-1/2" | 28-30 | — | 95-110 |
| Bowl, 7" x 11-3/4" (boat shaped) | 20-24 | 35-40 | 30-35 |
| Butter dish | 30-35 | 95-110 | 65-75 |
| Cake plate, 10-3/4" (footed) | 8-10 | 30-35 | 28-30 |
| Candlesticks, 3" (pair) | 24-26 | — | 75-85 |
| Candy jar and cover | 18-20 | — | 85-95 |
| Coaster, 3-1/4" | 4-6 | — | 16-18 |
| Compote | 10-12 | — | 28-30 |
| Creamer (2 styles) | 8-10 | 12-15 | 10-12 |
| Cup | 4-6 | 10-12 | 8-10 |
| Pitcher, 4-1/2" | 18-20 | — | 120-135 |
| Pitcher, 5" | 18-20 | — | — |
| Pitcher, 6-3/4" | 12-15 | 65-70 | 35-40 |
| Plate, 6" | 3-4 | 6-8 | 4-6 |
| Plate, 7" | 4-5 | 24-26 | 22-24 |
| Plate, 9" | 6-8 | 30-35 | 26-28 |
| Plate, sandwich, 10-1/4" (handled) | 8-10 | 18-20 | 16-20 |
| Plate, 13-5/8" (salver) | 14-16 | 35-40 | 30-35 |
| Platter, 11-1/2" (oval) | 8-10 | 26-28 | 24-26 |
| Relish platter, 11-1/2" (sectioned) | 12-14 | — | 195-220 |

| ITEM & DESCRIPTION | DOLLAR VALUE RANGES BY COLOR | | |
|---|---|---|---|
| | Crystal | Green | Pink |
| Salt and pepper (pair) | 18-20 | 55-65 | 40-45 |
| Saucer | 2-3 | 4-5 | 3-4 |
| Sherbet (footed) | 3-4 | 16-18 | 12-14 |
| Sugar and cover (3 styles) | 24-26 | 45-50 | 35-45 |
| Tray, 4" (square) | 5-6 | 12-15 | 10-12 |
| Tray, 4-1/8" x 9" | 5-6 | 12-15 | 10-12 |
| Tray, 8-1/2" x 9-3/4" (handled) | 8-10 | 30-35 | 26-28 |
| Tray, 8-1/2" x 9-3/4" (without handles) | 12-15 | — | 85-95 |
| Tumbler, 3-1/4" | 8-10 | 24-26 | 22-24 |
| Tumbler, 4" | 8-10 | 26-28 | 18-20 |
| Tumbler, 5" | 8-10 | 50-60 | 35-45 |
| Tumbler, 4" (footed) | 8-10 | — | — |
| Tumbler, 7-1/4" (footed) | 12-14 | — | — |

# PATTERN INDEX